To Amesha
Enjoy
Gerald
484-691-1363

MW01231535

Risking Paradise

A novel by

Gerald Randolph Howard

Publishing Associates, Inc.
Atlanta, GA 30310

Published in the United States of America by
Publishing Associates, Inc., Atlanta, Georgia.
ISBN: 978-0-942683-10-3 a trade paperback book.

For book orders, author appearance inquiries and interviews, contact the author at: www.riskingparadise.com

or the Publisher by mail at:
Publishing Associates, Inc.
5020 Montcalm Drive
Atlanta, Georgia 30331
Fcpublish@aol.com.

Library of Congress Cataloging In Publication Data

I dedicate this book to the loving memory of my mother, Delores Williams Howard. To my daughter, allow this to be evidence that you can do anything you put your mind to. My brothers, thank you for setting standards that challenge me. Our literary circle is now complete.

Negril, Jamaica

Chapter 1

If the clamor of the road-beaten vehicles doesn't arouse the dead, the chickens will. Little London is a parish about ten miles southeast of Negril, Jamaica, about halfway to another town called Sav-la-Mar. Ten years ago, when my infatuation with the island began, the road was very hard to travel. Potholes kept traffic at a reasonably slow speed. The hit and miss gravel created so much dust that any considerate driver would go but so fast. But that was ten years ago. With the influx of tourists and money, the government now provides better roads and services. Now, traffic races up and down the road attempting to compensate for other roads that are still in need of repair. The lifestyle is so completely different than mine that I find it fascinating. I've come to realize that beauty can be found in some of the simplest things.

My girlfriend Jacy, her father and niece live here. The house, by Jamaican standards, is adequate. It has three bedrooms, a kitchen, and a living room. The house was built of wood retrieved from houses flattened by a tornado about ten years ago. My presence, beginning three years ago, prompted Jacy to install a bathroom to accommodate what she thought was my "American" sophistication. I appreciate her doing this because my remembrance of the outhouse is not pleasant. Her embarrassment of guests using the strongly scented, outdoor facility appeared to outweigh my inconvenience. I never complained, but I guess she could see a distinct look on my face after nature took its course. At that time, the only inside running water, hot not included, was in the new addition, accessible only through Jacy's room. If you took a few steps out the back door, you would've entered the cooking shed. The detached extension to the kitchen was not such a bad idea because it didn't allow the rest of the house to get hot when someone was cooking. Jacy has since had the shed removed and connected an updated kitchen with running water. The house is not air-conditioned, a luxury we "Americans" have come to require. With the temperature usually very warm in the Caribbean, the windows are always open. Located about thirty feet off the main road to Sav-la-Mar, the noise of the traffic is abated sometimes, mostly in the middle of the night. This is the only house Jacy has ever known so she is used to it. My stays here are usually a week at most, so I basically have to tolerate it.

This particular morning, the wake up call came at about 5:30 a.m. Sounds of the native patois being spoken with extreme urgency were followed by wailing female voices.

"What is all the commotion about?" I curiously asked Jacy.

"Me tink a car has hit someone," she guessed.

It didn't take much longer to find out she was right. News of the accident spread throughout the neighborhood. A neighbor knocked immediately on the door to validate news that we already had. The late delivery prompted Jacy to exit the house for no reason I could fathom. "Sweetheart, I'd prefer that you not go outside. I doubt that there is anything that you can do for the fellow."

Jacy looked at me and pleaded. "But Gee, him might be someone dat me know."

"Baby the condition of a twisted, bloody, body is not a sight that you should implant in your mind's eye to have to deal with later. I know you are concerned, but stay inside okay?"

"No problem mon."

A second knock took precedence and out the door she went.

I thought, "Damn... what a way to start the day on an island in the sun."

Little London is such a small parish that Jacy couldn't help but know the injured person lying twisted and exposed on the ground. It was a man who had helped on her bathroom addition. The story was that the poor fellow had been dragged beneath a car and came to rest fifty feet from the house. As I peered out the window, I could see Jacy looking at me looking at her. I thought someone should at least cover the body. The body layed exposed until an emergency crew showed up an hour later.

The unfortunate occurrence of someone being hit by a car is more likely to happen here than in the U.S. Cars are a luxury, so the general mode of transportation is by foot. Far too often, pedestrians were struck by cars. So much so that Jacy and others in the community were immune to the shock and horror of an auto accident on that narrow winding road. By 6:45 a.m., we had dozed off again.

By 7:30 a.m., we were taking advantage of a man's normal early morning arousal. Sometimes I wonder just how much noise can be heard throughout the creaky little house. Do Jacy's father and niece discuss the blow-by-blow details of what happens just a few feet away, or do they politely refrain from mentioning it, in consideration for their own privacy? Jacy and I always try to be as discreet as possible, but there are climactic periods of lovemaking that defy silence. During those periods, my fervent wish is that a thunderously loud truck would come barreling down the road at the same time as I do. I remember us laughing after one such vigorous occasion. We thought it was hilarious that a huge truck would rattle the house at the exact same time that we rattled the bed.

At 8:00 a.m. in the morning, a cold shower is hard to take. What should I do, immerse only my face or just jump in and get it over with? I try to grin and bear it. After a no air-conditioned lovemaking session, I have to do something. Even if the session is not an earth-shattering ten on the Richter scale, I wonder how anyone can go anywhere with the familiar smell of *poonany* hovering around his body. Not me, not the kid! So cold shower, like Marvin Gaye would sing, "let's get it on." After the initial shock, it's all good. Cleanliness is, after all, the next thing to Godliness. Plus, it doesn't tell everyone your business.

Jacy always has a cup of tea in the morning. She might fix me a dish of watermelon, pineapple, or mango fresh from a tree in her yard. Since I try to be health conscious, I appreciate it much better than the greasy fried eggs we Americans typically eat in the morning.

It's now 8:30 A.M. and Jacy has to leave for work. Even at this early hour, the sun feels like we are in for another balmy day.

We do our best to hide under the few trees located in the front of the house. On this morning, the road holds a blood-splattered reminder of the earlier tragedy. We have to catch a route taxi which is differentiated from other vehicles by it's license plate. A wave of the hand lets the driver know that we are going in his direction. A lot of people have to use the few there are, so they're usually full by the time we get to our destination. The repairs made to the roads leading to Negril make the trip more comfortable than before. The cabstand is the central stop. All sorts of road-weary cars are here jostling for position to load up and go again. Drivers shout out their destinations, obnoxiously aggressive in the battle to get patrons. From this cabstand, we can either walk to our destination or take another taxi. The naturalness of the island abounds. By this time, usually a few minutes before nine, the comfort of the morning shower (if you took one) has worn off. It's not unusual to be reminded that everyone is not as conscious about personal hygiene as you might be.

Jacy works in a cambio, which is a lotto ticket sales booth that also changes foreign money. Her present location is within walking distance of the cabstand.

I met Jacy while she was working and I was on a previous trip to Jamaica, one of my favorite vacation spots. There are some chairs under an awning at the west end cambio, which adjoins a restaurant. Quite often the employees of both places might be seen there relaxing.

My rowdy friends and I usually rent a vehicle on our adventures; therefore we can go anywhere at our leisure. The group consisted of Hakeem, his brother Robbie, Freddy and myself; all employees/relatives/friends.

Even though Hakeem and Robbie are brothers, they are as different as night and day. Hakeem, the younger of the two, is much more aggressive than his brother. He also works for me and is my right-hand-man. Oftentimes, I have to remind him that I, as the boss, have executive privilege when it comes to final decisions. At twenty-six, his interests rest in rap music and low-rider trucks.

Robbie, a few years older, is not as accomplished. A good looking, small man, he mumbles when he talks, and I have to ask him constantly to repeat himself. Robbie always invites us to go out to the after-hour clubs that he frequents, but we never accept his invitations. The odd thing about Robbie is that despite being thirty plus, he still lives with his mother. I have no idea why because she is quite capable of taking care of herself.

Freddy's crude and rudeness is so obviously funny, that it keeps a permanent, self conscious smile on his face. I think he flunked manners 101. Freddy came straight out of "da hood." He claims confusion about who his father is, which appears to have been a white man. His "good hair" and fair skin have always been his attention getters. Although the four of us are often caught displaying degrees of stupidity, Freddy is the textbook definition of a buckethead.

The four of us have a pact that if any of us hit the lottery, none of us will ever have to work again. Our musketeer motto is, "all for one and one for all."

The day I met Jacy, Hakeem was driving. She just happened to be sitting in one of the chairs out front of the cambio. Now, of course, a Brotha is going to notice a pretty face and long hair. I scoped Jacy and immediately noticed a window of opportunity. One of my mottos is this: "When you see the window of opportunity open, you only have so much time before it closes." So, no sooner had I glanced in Jacy's direction, I shouted, "Honey alert, turn this bad boy around Hakeem!"

Freddy turned and asked, "You see some beef Gee?"

I scolded, "No, Freddy, I see something pretty that interests me. I've told you about using that 'beef' word."

Amongst our gang it's a rule that if you go through all the trouble of turning around to see some honey, you have to speak. You got to get yo' Mack on. I have yet to lose my player's license, nor has it ever been revoked for any period of time. I have been put on probation a time or two. But if my quest was to be the undisputed heavyweight player of the world, I've incurred no major offenses. I haven't bitten off any ears in the heat of passion, nor have I caught anything that a Monday morning visit to a doctor's office couldn't cure. So, by the time we had driven back to the point of attack, the boys had pumped me up and I had rehearsed my lines. Every situation determines what line to use. If I'm feeling silly (which I usually am), my impromptu ghetto voice might say something like "Yo, what yo' name is, girl?" By the time we had driven back, I had glimpsed the calm, serene look on this pretty face. Not thinking my usual approach would work, I employed a simple, "Hello, how are you?"

The pretty face replied, "Fine, tank you."

I volunteered my name. "I'm Grant Howell."

She showed a pretty set of teeth and replied. "I'm Jacy Weber." I detected a subtle attempt to mock me.

"Everyone calls me Gee."

For some reason, a polite but aggressive, "Come here," came out of my mouth. Now ain't that some junk? These siditty-ass Americans swearing up and down they're "the stuff," have the audacity to think that American smack works everywhere. To my surprise, Jacy calmly got up and walked over to our car. The tidbits of small talk I really don't remember. I was too enthralled by the view of two luscious breasts exposing themselves to my line of vision. I had to talk fast because my three comrades would soon put in their two cents if given the opportunity. You see, all is fair in love and war and everybody knows the rules. Until the lady chooses you, it's all fair game.

"So how long are you guys going to be visiting?" Jacy inquired.

We did have the look of tourists. "What makes you think we're visiting?"

"First of all, your license plates give you away, all de rental cars have blue ones. Udda den yo accents, de cameras are official tourist paraphernalia. Me live here, gentlemen. Me know who be who."

I felt like I had just gotten jabbed by Ali. I thought, "Okay Gee, what makes you think you can come at this girl and not be on your toes?" She was very calm and reserved, her demeanor unrehearsed. I'm the one who had the time to spot her and turn around; I should've gotten myself together.

"We'll be here three more days," I replied. The gang still hadn't managed to get any words in.

"Well, me hope you enjoy your stay and you find whatever it is you're looking for."

Jacy's straight teeth caught my attention. I thought, "pretty face, hair, and straight teeth, too." Surely her nonchalance to her revealed breasts must have something to do with the island's natural atmosphere. Known to say and do some bucket-headed things, without thinking of the consequences, I said, "I'm looking for a wife, someone that looks, walks and talks just like you." I gave her my best smile.

Jacy was still on her toes. "Dere's a jewelry store just beyond de roundabout, and we can go pick out someting as soon as me get off."

All of a sudden, the Three Stooges were rolling around laughing, slap'n and dap'n in this hot car knowing darn well I had just put my foot in my mouth. I was lost for words. Those clowns knew that, at times, I got my words a little mixed up. My best reply to the pretty islander sounded something like "Wella... wella... alright... ah.... ah.... you.... you." In the midst of my stuttering, and the stooges weren't making it any easier for me to find a good comeback, one managed to contain his laughter long enough to offer to loan me a few hundred till we got back to the States. The other two looked like they might pee their pants any minute.

Rule 22 of the "How-To-Save-Face" handbook flashed into my head out of nowhere. Change the subject. "Are you having a good day today, Ms. Jacy?"

Jacy couldn't contain her laughter. Directing her attention to Freddy, the only stooge in control of himself, she asked, "where did you get dis guy?"

"Since he's the only one with a credit card we let him

come with us this time." Had Jacy known that this was about my tenth trip and Freddy's first, I had a feeling she wouldn't have let him get away with that.

"Oh, so Gee is de stable one of de group." Jacy was on a roll now. At this point, I was really surprised that what appeared to be just another pretty face was really quite a sharp woman. I appreciate mature folk, you learn more. "How old are you, Gee?"

I invoked another rule. "How old do I look?" The stooges had regained some composure.

A smile lit Jacy's face. This gave her the opportunity to look me up and down. She gave me a total once over and made an educated guess. "You somewhere in yo thirties." The gang knew how far off she was. I can only attribute my youthful looks to the hardworking occupation I had chosen twenty years earlier. Owning my own household furniture moving business was not totally my choice. I had gotten a two-year degree after I came out of the Army, and operating a computer just didn't satisfy my youthful financial ambitions. One of my brothers, a struggling musician at the time, supplemented his gigs with small moving jobs. He'd move washers and dryers, couches, or whatever he could get in his van. I placed an ad in the newspaper, and the next thing I knew, I was working all the time, making more in a day than I had operating a computer all week. It was an easy decision to go full time. The hard, physical labor didn't bother me. I had been practicing karate for about six years, so I just looked at it as another workout, one that paid. The money spoiled me.

"Wow aren't you flattering! You know that will get you everywhere." I always felt I should play flattered when people guessed my age so far off. I had experienced this many times before and genuinely felt good that I didn't look my age. But who wouldn't? "Girl," I said in a stereotypical black voice. "You made my day. No, you made my week; I'm forty-six."

"Yeah right, mon." Jacy exclaimed. "You know what happens when you lie to a Jamaican? We have powers, you know. Me can help you look forty-six if you want to be dat old." Her girlish grin was appealing.

"Tell her, Hakeem," I insisted.

"Yup, he's an old man all right. His bald head is no attempt to keep up with the styles. My partner's hair-growing days were over long ago," Hakeem said.

Jacy declared, "Well, whatever root juice you be drinking, keep it up."

"It's not root juice, pretty lady. It's just a big dose of hard work everyday. As a matter of fact how old are you? Or is it not proper to ask a lady that?"

Now I know that generally women don't like telling their age, but either this pretty islander was going to tell or not.

"Twenty-seven," she offered without hesitation.

I appreciated not going through a bunch of changes about it.

"Girl, I got a daughter twenty-four."

"Are you married?"

"No, I haven't been married for quite a while. But I think it's kind of funny that I have a child who's almost your age."

"If she is twenty-four, she's definitely no child? Does she know you always be flirtin' wit young girls?"

"Who says I'm flirting? Besides, if I was, I had no idea how old you were."

"Well, Mr. Gee, if you not flirting den why you turn yo car around and come back?"

"How do you know we turned around?"

"Oh, me saw dat pretty bald head of yours de first time you went by. De sun came through de window and bounced right off yo head. It almost blinded me, Mon."

My gang got a kick out of that. Why did she have to give the peanut gallery something to feed on? It provided temporary entertainment. They needed that. But, I could see they were getting a little anxious to leave.

13

"Well, I know you are working so we won't interrupt you any more," I said.

"Oh, you not interrupting me."

"It sure would be a pleasure to stop by some other time, maybe tomorrow if you don't mind?"

"It's okay, don't you guys get in too much trouble," directing that comment to my boys.

"Have a wonderful day, Ms. Jacy, I hope to see you later." As we drove off to look for the next points of interest, I turned and caught her looking. I blew a kiss that brought a smile and exposed those pretty teeth again.

Freddy was the first to start the ribbing. "Man! What you smiling at? That young lady is looking for a husband too. A free trip to the land of milk and honey, ain't nut'n new."

"Oh, I can't smile if I want to?"

Hakeem added his two cents, "You old men get a kick out of playing with them young, fine, sexy little mommas, don't ya?" Everyone broke out laughing.

"I can't be too old, Buckethead, these eyes I got were the first to spot her. Besides, you just hatin' cause you got no rap."

"Negro please, you know who the mack-daddy-est rapper in Atlanta G-A is," Hakeem replied.

Robbie, the reeferhead, interjected, "Hey man, did I see one of the beef's eyes looking east while the other was looking west?" Robbie's wisecrack did verify a hunch that Jacy appeared to have a problem with one of her eyes.

"Man, I couldn't take my eyes off those pretty breasts long enough to look at her eyes," I said.

"Honey alert. Honey alert!" Freddy yelled.

This time, it was Freddy with the eagle eyes. This is how we spent our days in paradise, enjoying all the pretty native sights, be it sand, sun, or anything else that caught our attention. Jacy had caught mine and I was already looking for an excuse to get away from the clowns so I could enjoy that pretty young lady's company again.

Having come to Jamaica several times has given me a feel for what is going on. There are plenty of tourist attractions, if that's what you want. The island has enough commercial places to accommodate any tourist. Being a black American, I appreciate seeing black faces in such a different atmosphere. Jamacian blacks live a very different life than American blacks. If I were to make a relative guess, I would say that living in Jamaica today is like living in the U.S. in the 1940s. It's akin to living in a small West Virginia town. If there's no running water in your house, either you get it from the river, your neighbor's faucet, or maybe the community source that has been trucked in. In Jamaica, it's not out of the ordinary to see someone balancing a bucket of water on the top of their head. Bringing water might be the chore of even the smallest family members. To be honest, I feel life is hard in the hot, tropical sun, even though it's a vacationer's destination.

Scene after scene reminds me of the struggling history of Black people. Here, struggling is still a way of life. Over the years, I've enjoyed venturing away from the tourist spots and interacting with the "real" people. I love the accents. To listen to the girls talk and feel their country innocence is endearing to me. I get the feel of having a personal relationship with each one that permits my handshake to linger. I imagine my American accent is a novelty to them just as theirs is to me.

In the old men, you can't help but see years of hard work. Being natural family providers, life seems hardest on the men. They look weary and worn, yet they still have to work. I wonder who takes care of these old guys when they can't work the fields anymore? There are very few jobs and many people. In the U.S., the life expectancy of a black male is about sixty-nine years old. I wonder what it is in Jamaica. What do these people, living in these little huts, do for medical care? The man who was hit by the car in front of Jacy's house verified what I already knew. Medical emergencies can turn into life-threatening situations. There is no telling how many of the women are having babies with no professional medical assistance whatsoever. My travels have given me the perspective to understand the differences. My willingness for adventure draws me to Jamaica. I love this place. I wish I could come more often.

15

Gerald Randolph Howard

A Second Look

Jacy's trip home is another round of cab hopping. She either walks or takes a cab to the central cabstand, where she takes another to Little London. Sometimes she gets lucky and arranges a ride with a friend she might encounter during her day at work. Saving the cab fare makes life a little easier. A route taxi charges about seventy-five cents. For Jacy, that's a dollar and a half a day. She sometimes spends $7.50 a week for cab fare. With the unemployment rate being so high, Jamaicans are fortunate to have a job. Consequently, the wages are terrible. Jacy makes about ninety dollars a week. Ninety dollars is not much in either the U.S. or Jamaica. But, if Jacy didn't have the job, someone else would. There aren't many alternatives. There are jobs in the tourist industry, which usually means some type of subservient, unskilled labor. Those jobs pay comparably the same. On her job, she constantly counts money, making her math skills very sharp.

Jacy's father, whom I respectfully call Mr. Weber, is in his sixties and unemployed. He hurt his leg in an on-the-job accident several years ago that ended his career. He has recuperated from his injury but unfortunately there is no demand for a sixty-something year old man with no marketable skills. A tall, frail man, he does what he can around the house to contribute. He receives no disabilitiy or pension. I have had interesting man-to-man conversations with Mr. Weber. His strong Jamaican accent makes me have to really listen carefully to understand the points he tries to make. Although we have had a number of occasions to talk, I'm sure he has much more to share. Mr. Weber is my peer, from another place and time, and I find him fascinating to talk to.

Mika is Jacy's niece and Mr. Weber's granddaughter. She lives at the house as a matter of convenience. I'm not sure how long this arrangement has been this way, but it is obvious that Jacy and Mika are close. I've observed their loving interactions much like a mother and daughter would have. I have met Mika's biological mother and father. They are fine people, but there is just no room in their one room apartment for Mika. In reality, it is a sectioned-off room in someone's house. I was surprised to see how crowded it was. I dropped Mika off there once and I don't understand why Mika's Father doesn't to get a bigger place. In the eight grade, I understand Mika is an outstanding student. Much of that credit can be given to Jacy for the attention she gives to Mika's schoolwork.

Jacy is the sole provider of the household. The responsibility of providing for her father and niece, I would speculate, has got to be tough. She likes to read romance novels. She gets them from a male friend that works in a hotel. From what I can tell, this person is a possible suitor who watches out for her, as best he can. I never really inquired. Her room is filled with books. We've all seen images of sunbathing tourists reading on the beach. I guess some figure it's better to leave them in their rooms rather than take them back home. Consequently, these books keep her reading skills up. I would even go so far as to say they provide her with a form of escape. Needless to say, Jacy is a very bright young lady. She is well-spoken and surprises me with her wittiness.

I used a jogging session as a second occasion to cross paths with her. It was kind of hard getting started. Partying at Risky Business, a beach club, til' one a.m. had something to do with it. There was plenty of music, women, and whatever else you might want to sample. Oh, I'm not one to sit back and let everyone else have all the fun. I danced and grooved to the pure reggae beats, flirted with the pretty ladies until some mentioned money. Hakeem drank his nerve up and Freddy was steadily pulling out his wallet. Now my buddy Robbie is a strange cat; he seemed more interested in getting high and hanging with the white boys from the U.S. Another motto of mine is: "If I haven't done what I'm gonna do by twelve, I am not gonna do it." I stayed longer than usual 'cause the band was jammin'. Risky Business is within walking distance of the Treehouse, the hotel where I usually stay. I left earlier than the gang did. I never have been one to stay out all night long.

Personally, I can't see coming to a place this beautiful and sleeping all day. The morning breeze off the ocean is delightfully clean and the view clears my head. My previous day's encounter with Jacy swirled through my head. I was having the hardest time remembering her name. I used to attribute my bad memory to reefer. They say it kills your memory brain cells. I had stopped smoking the stuff two years earlier, yet the effects lingered. Always gorging myself with food after smoking and feeling stupid for hours, I got tired of being tired of it. So I quit. Now I'm wondering why I still have a bad memory. Well, even if I couldn't remember her name, I remembered where she worked, and she did say I could stop by to say hello. I figured it was about three miles away. I've always bragged that I could run five miles any day of the week. So I thought, "why not?" I turned in between a couple of beachfront hotels and headed in that direction. If she was three miles away I figured I'd be well into it, drenching wet with sweat as I arrived. A Lady friend once told me, "Ladies like to see a Brotha sweat, whether it is on top of them or on the job. Sweating shows that you can "hang." So surely I can get my foot in the door if she sees that I'm in good physical condition.

I don't care if it's six in the morning or six in the evening — it's always hot in Jamaica. It didn't take much to break a sweat, so by the time I made the last corner to the cambio, I had a good one going. Feeling playful, I ran past the store as if Jacy weren't there. The door was open, so I knew someone was. I needed to do something unique to catch her attention. Like a movie being played backwards, I stopped in my tracks about ten feet past the place, and started back peddling on the path I had just covered. I stopped again and returned over the same trail five or six times. Anyone watching would've sworn I was crazy. Out of the corner of my eye, I saw a body appear.

"Excuse me Sir, me tink you'd better stop. De sun is getting to you," Jacy yelled at me.

I acted like I didn't hear her.

"Hello Sir, would you please stop, you're getting my street all wet wit your perspiring," she called again.

"Oh... good morning," I acted as if I was surprised she was talking to me. "How are you today?"

She replied, "Fine, why you up so early?"

19

By this time, I had brought my drenched self over to her door. "Early, early?" I said in a playful voice. "Girl... It's almost nine o'clock. I've been half way 'round the world and back."

"Yeah right, and me name be Cleopatra."

"I would have run the rest of the way but I wanted to save some energy for when I got to see you again. You did say I could stop and see you, remember?"

"Me vaguely remember someting like dat. Me didn't tink it would be so soon, like dis."

"This might be a little soon, but this isn't such an odd circumstance. You might see me doing anything. Tomorrow, you might see me flying a helicopter overhead."

"And me last name be Kennedy."

I scratched my head and pretended to be thinking. "Are you related to the infamous presidential Kennedy family?" I asked, knowing that a black Jamaican was far removed from the white American dynasty.

"Oh... Me didn't tell you?"

"Well I doubt that your name is Cleopatra Kennedy. To be honest with you, I was so impressed by your good looks yesterday, your name didn't really sink into my head."

"Well Mr. Gee, you brain not in as good condition as your body huh? Why me get all de knuckleheads?"

"Oh, so I'm a knucklehead cause I didn't remember your name?"

"Yup."

"Dang... you didn't call me a knucklehead."

"Yes me did."

Most generally, when I jog, I don't stop until I've done the designated number of miles I had set out to do. Making an exception this time, I was really killing two birds with one stone. One, coming back to see Jacy so quickly should have told her I was interested. Two, I wanted her to see me sweat. I wanted her to see that I could hang.

"Anyway, Miss, I'm on a mission, so let me keep going. I hope you have a wonderful day, and by the way, what is your name again?"

"Tell you what Gee, if me see you again, me tell you. If me don't see you, it wouldn't be dat important."

"Dang... no you didn't put me off like that."

"Yes me did."

As I got back into my jog, I made my stride look as pretty as possible. About fifteen yards away I felt my booty alarm go off. I turned around, back peddling, to see her eyes trained directly at my butt. I blew a kiss and got another smile. Thinking, "Yo, Gee, it's on now."

By the time I got back to the Treehouse, the peanut gallery still hadn't gotten up. I showered, hung my wet clothes out to dry, and started breakfast. I know these clowns well enough to know that the smell of food cooking will wake them up. So, as usual, I threw enough on for everybody. I always make it clear that if I cook, somebody else has to clean up. This ought to be understood, but usually the three stooges peddle around, goof off, and do such a half-ass job that I have to finish. As I was cooking, a couple of scantily clad young ladies started ducking in and out of the bathroom. It didn't take long to figure out what had happened the night before. I hadn't noticed any new bodies as I headed out the door a couple of hours ago but I also hadn't knocked on any doors to invite anyone to join me. Like I said, I know them. They never accept my invitations, so I don't waste my time anymore. Shapely, half-dressed booties scurried around, towels barely covering breasts, and the three stooges finally appeared, one by one.

"Is it soup yet?" Hakeem asked sleepily.

"You got to get it while the gettin's good," I replied. I fixed a plate for myself and washed it down with a big glass of milk. "Ah...I love milk." The beach was waiting.

There are always some folks sunbathing or doing something down by the water. Either I sat alone in peace or found someone to talk to. On some occasions, spontaneous conversations sprang up with strangers. Hotel personnel might be sweeping leaves off the sand. Waiters or waitresses might be preparing the open-air restaurant. So there was always someone around to mess with. One of the groundskeepers was a native Jamaican named Robert. We'd developed somewhat of a friendship over the years that I had stayed at the Treehouse. Robert was about twenty-one years old with a rather muscular build developed from his few years of obvious hard work. On my morning jogs I playfully invited him to join me, knowing he had to work. He always playfully responded, "next time." But Robert was starting to bug me. He had learned to "hustle" the tourist. Consequently, I found myself avoiding the naive young man that I had seen evolve into something else.

"Yo, Robert, what's up?"

"Respect Gee, everyting cool?"

"Yeah everything's cool, just getting my day started."

"Me see you when you started out jogging. You know, me wanted to go wit you today..."

"Yeah right, Robert, you always say that."

"Me really really was dis time, Mon. Me feel like about five or six miles today."

"Well, you missed out 'cause I did about those many today. I ran down to the cambio in the West End and back."

"Yeah, me know de place, de Root Lady be dere sometimes."

"I don't know anything about the Root Lady, but I did see a fine, young and sexy thing there this morning."

"You have to be careful, Mon, sometimes de beef take control of you in ways you don't understand."

"Like I see you take control of these older ladies around here."

I chuckled at Robert's reference to women. "Man, where did you get that word 'beef' from? Sounds like you been talking to some of my gang."

"Yeah Gee, dem some funny guys, mon."

"Call them 'ladies' Robert, it sounds better."

"Yeah, Mon, da ladies always be around. All you have to do is keep your eyes open."

"Okay, I'll keep my eyes open, and try to beat you to them."

"No, Mon, dere's enough to go around for everybody. You take de young ladies. Dey don't want to spend no money. Me take de older ones. Dey got plenty to spend."

"It's called the window of opportunity, Robert."

"Huh?"

"When the window of opportunity is open you only have so much time before it closes."

"Dat make good sense to me, Mon." I gave Robert a high five. I was downwind as he raised his armpit high. Whew! Wish I could've taken that one back.

"Look here Robert, you been here long enough to know what's happening."

"Yeah, de young ones are nice to look at but de older ones be needing some attention. All you have to do is be nice to dem and dey be nice to you, Gee. Me special friend say she going to help me go in de boating business. Me show tourists around and stuff."

"I hear you, Bro."

"Yo, Gee, me need you to do me a favor."

"What's that, Robert?"

"Me need a cell phone."

"Robert!" I looked at him like he was crazy. "What the hell you need a cell phone for? Sounds like you need to get one of them old girls to get you one of those, too. Besides, I told you about trying to hustle me."

"No, Mon, why you say dat? Me not trying to hustle you," he said with a chuckle.

"See, you can't even deny it with a straight face. All right, brotha, it's time to go back to work." I gave him some more dap but held back on the hug that usually goes with it. I was still downwind. I headed over to a thatched roof gazebo to cool out for a while.

With the morning breeze coming off the ocean, there couldn't be a more peaceful place. The sun was kick'n but I found a nice shady spot. I had nowhere to go and another whole day to get there. What more could a brotha want? This was the furthest place from my regular routine. No trucks to pull maintenance on. No employees calling in late. No customers calling at all hours of the day and night. This atmosphere was so different than life in the U.S., which made me appreciate it even more. Another motto of mine is, "Life is what you make it. If you aren't enjoying it, it's nobody's fault but your own." The picture-perfect scenario soon lulled me into a deep sleep, dreaming of the fine, sexy thing I had my mind's eye on.

An hour or so later, Freddy, Hakeem, and Robbie finally surfaced with the two ladies they had met the night before. I didn't know who was with whom or who did what to whom. The girls' nighttime attire told me that I thought maybe they had all shared whatever the girls were selling.

"All right, Hakeem," I whispered. "You know the routine, why you dragging them out here. You messing up any play we might get from the legit ladies."

"Man, I just came to tell you we gonna run them home and be right back."

"That's cool, watermelon head," I said with aggravation in my voice. "Bye."

"Like I said, we'll be right back."

I would never come this far and not take the opportunity to enjoy the ocean, so I jumped in. It was somewhere around noon because the sun was dead overhead. This would be my second exercise session of the day. It took the gang about an hour to get back.

"Yo, Gee, what's up?" Hakeem called to me as he jumped into a nice-sized wave.

"You da Man."

"Naw, you da Man."

"Naw, I'm da Man standing next to da Man."

"What's up?"

"I said you da Man."

"Nothing, just chill'n."

"Just chill'n man?"

"Yup, just chill'n. We're getting ready to go jerk some chicken. You wanna hang?"

"I got a chicken y'all can jerk right now, if you want sump'n to jerk."

"Look you know what I mean, you hang'n or not?"

"Didn't y'all just get through eating a little while ago?"

We both climbed out of the water and headed towards the gazebo.

"Shoot... dem young beef killed that stuff you cooked. Looked like they hadn't eaten in a couple of days."

"They probably hadn't. They hit you in the wallet?"

"Boy, you done bumped yo head," Hakeem snorted. "You know the kid don't play that. Now if Robbie and Freddy gave up the duckies, that's a different story. But you know the kid ain't giving up nut'n but big bang and bubblegum... And I'm fresh out of bubblegum."

I grabbed my towel to dry myself off and said, "Let's ride."

There is nothing more Jamaican than jerk chicken. There are basically two choices. Either you can go to a Mom and Pop-type place, someone's house converted to a restaurant, or you can jerk some from one of the roadside venders. In either case, I doubt that the FDA inspectors visit often. With that in mind, you just bless the food real good and go for what you know. There were a couple of favorite spots we preferred to jerk. Marla's, the Mom and Pop variety, was in the West End. We usually hit the street vendors late at night on the way in from the beach clubs. I always had to have a little alcohol to dull my rational thinking, because I knew darn well these guys didn't have food handler permits. At least at the Mom and Pop places there was running water to clean something. The boys jerking in the street didn't have dookie. Marla's was just past Jacy's cambio.

As we neared the restaurant, I said, "Yo, Homeskillet, swing up to the cambio for a minute and let me yell at this honey. It won't take me long."

Freddy spoke up. "Damn, Bro, you got it bad, don't you?"

"What you talking 'bout man, it ain't gonna take but a minute." No one was aware that I had just seen her a couple of hours earlier.

Robbie, with his dope smoking booty added, "Alright man, take a good look at those eyes this time and you'll see what I was talk'n about."

>"Take a look at these nuts, Robbie and you'll see what I'm talk'n about."

>"All right Gee, remember we're going to get something to eat," Hakeem said.

>"If y'all wouldn't have had those ladies of the evening in the room this morning, you'd have had something to eat, Homebox. Why y'all trip'n? I said I'll only be a minute."

Hakeem, who was driving, accommodated my request and pulled up right to the front door. I got out and went in, letting Jacy see my face. I figured that would let her know I had come to see her. To my surprise, the two young ladies that stayed the night with the boys were in line. It appeared as though they were exchanging American money over to Jamaican. I nodded acknowledgement to them. I walked back to the car, giving my new friend the liberty to join me at her convenience. The panoramic view of the ocean from here was great. I could smell it. The car's air conditioner wasn't the greatest, but it was more comfortable than the afternoon heat. I started to mention to the fellas that there were some familiar faces inside, but by the time I seated one butt cheek in the car, Jacy was in the doorway.

>"Good afternoon," I offered, "I hope we're not interrupting you?"

Freddy in the back seat with me whispered under his breath, "Look, man, ask her if she is going to give you some poonanny so we can go get something to eat."

"Damn, Freddy, you been chewing on yo socks again?"

Jacy spoke with a hint of surprise. "To what do I owe a second visit in less than four hours?" She pretended to look at an imaginary watch.

"Uh-oh," I thought. "She just exposed my previous rendezvous to the knuckleheads." They put two and two together in unison.

Robbie busted out with a long drawn-out, "Ah ha..."

Freddy said, "Damn, boy, you got it bad!"

I quietly shot back at Freddy. "Naw, Freddy, yo breath is bad!" I had to wait for the carload to calm down to continue my conversation.

I directed my attention back to Jacy. "You must be living right to receive so many blessings in so short period of time," I said. Standing by the car, the sun shone straight through her dress, making it hard to look her steadily in the eyes.

She replied, "Yes, me probably living right, but as me tell you, me have powers, you know. To tell de trut, I put a spell on you."

"If you keep telling me that I might start to believe you."

"Me got a drop of your sweat you left on me doorstep. Me mixed it with de perfume me have. Me surprised it took you so long to come back." She leaned over and whispered in my ear, "You see, you no choose Jacy, Mr. Gee..., Jacy choose you."

Leaning close to me, she touched her index finger to my shoulder. Such a chill came over my whole body that Freddy gave me a strange look. Jacy took a step back and directed her attention to the guys up front. "You all had a good time at Risky Business last night."

Robbie looked at Hakeem, then turned back to Jacy. "That was a statement, not a question. Oh, you saw us there last night?"

"No. Me don't have to see you to know you had a good time."

Robbie volunteered, "I can't speak for everyone, but I had a ball."

"And you Gee, you find what you be looking for?"

Before I could answer, the phone rang in the cambio. Jacy hurried to answer it, meeting the two female customers at the door. Their attention was riveted on splitting up their change. Freddy spoke, "Hello pretty ladies." As they strolled over to the car, I got out. Since the girls were there, the fellas would be temporarily entertained and I could talk to Jacy. I went into the cambio and waited until Jacy finished the call.

"I knew your name was Jacy, I just couldn't remember your last name."

"Yeah right! You still tinking me name was Cleopatra Kennedy."

"Well, it would be nice if you had the Kennedy money."

"Yes, but me not dat lucky. Me last name is Weber. Now write it down so you won't forget it dis time."

"Jacy Weber... Jacy Weber... Jacy Weber...There, I just wrote it down in my head. It will remain there forever."

"So which one of dem girls did you have last night?"

"What?" I said expressively.

"Don't deny it. Me saw dem coming out of your hotel room."

"Liar, liar pants on fire. You heard them talking about that little chump change you converted for them. I'll bet they saw our car pull up and started talking. You aren't fooling me. To tell the truth I didn't even know they were in the room until this morning when I came back from jogging."

"Yeah right, and me name is Cleo..."

I interrupted before she got a chance to finish. "Girl, how you think I have enough energy to get up and exercise the way I do if I'm prowling throughout the night? Hey, look, when I'm out, if I don't do what I'm gonna do by twelve o'clock, I ain't gonna do it. I came in last night and was knocked out when they got in. I didn't know what they were up to. The first hint that I had of those girls was this morning when I started cooking breakfast. Now if you don't believe that Ms. Kennedy, I mean Weber, I guess I got nothing to say to you."

"See, you forget me name already. I get all de knuckleheads; and your friends dey trouble. You shouldn't hang around dem."

"And I didn't forget your name so don't start that again," I replied.

The phone rang again. I browsed around to kill some time while the girls had the guys going. Jacy waited on a customer while she spoke on the phone. I couldn't understand a word of her patois.

"Yo, Homeskillet." Freddy called out. "Let's ride."

I think Jacy offered to call the person on the phone back later as she finished with the customer. "Okay pretty girl, I'm going to have to talk to you later. I'm not finished with you, besides you got to tell me what you just did to me."

"Me not finished wit you either, and what you talking about, 'what me just did to you?'"

By now, the peanut gallery had run out of patience and was honking the horn.

"Like I said, I'm not finished with you." I blew her a kiss as I hit the door. The pretty lady stood up from behind her desk and smiled.

Throw 'n Down

Chapter 3

"Damn," I thought. "I sure like to eat."

If I didn't exercise so much I'd be as big as a house. The cook at Marla's jerked the hell out of this chicken. It's a good thing there weren't any single ladies around 'cause we were throwing down. Our manners were left somewhere else. Robbie's and Hakeem's excuse for stuffing themselves like pigs could be blamed on their last joint. Freddy and I were enjoying the food for its genuine goodness. We all ate something different, from oxtails to jerk chicken. Immersed in our own tasty worlds, we were startled by an impromptu visit from a local Rasta man. The Rastas are a conscientious sect. Be it through eating or personal care, their conscientiousness is manifested through natural living. Many refuse to use deodorants or even take pills. This particular fellow obviously didn't use deodorant, because homeboy was kick'n. This guy had more funks than Bootsy and Slick Rick put together. He was trying to sell us on the virtues of his homemade bottle of root juice.

> "Listen, Mon, me got de ting you need. Dis is me special brew. It make yo nature stand up like a donkey, Mon," he explained.

If foreigners spoke as fast or used as much slang as Jamaicans, they would misunderstand what we say as much as we misunderstand what they say.

Hakeem turned his attention to Freddy and said, "I wish homeboy would roll his funky booty somewhere else before he makes me stand up and leave." These two clowns were always cutting up. Freddy had gotten a whiff of the funk, and was making a stupid face. I could see the clowning getting started. It just so happened that Robbie, with his high ass, was taking a sip of Red Stripe beer and chuckling at Hakeem's comment at exactly the wrong time. Before I knew it, beer was going everywhere, out of his mouth and nose.

"Man, what an embarrassment," I thought.

A romantic couple next to us looked on with astonishment. Hakeem's and Freddy's foolishness, compounded by the mess Robbie was making, had me laughing hysterically. The sight of beer coming out of Robbie's nose reminded me of a similar incident I'd had with milk back in high school. I was laughing so hard, tears were coming out of my eyes. A stomach full of jerk chicken and Red Stripe didn't make matters any better. Neither did the lack of fresh air caused by our uninvited visitor. Hakeem was the only one in control of himself, and was eating as if nothing was happening. He looked up at the dreadlocked fellow and said with a straight face, "No, sir, I think we'll all be too full from this good food for anything else."

Evidently Hakeem's response was good enough to ward off the poor fellow. I think he was looking for a reason to leave, and that was sufficient.

"Oh, by the way Gee," Hakeem said. "You going to eat the rest of that rice you got over there?"

I couldn't answer. Freddy and Robbie were still trying to get themselves together. So for the next few minutes, we just sat there looking stupid at each other looking stupid, rubbing our stomachs, and trying to get Hakeem to shut up.

Eventually we managed to pay our bill and leave. We left a bigger tip than usual to make up for the commotion.

T'ree-part Harmony

Chapter 4

This was the last of our seven days in paradise. It was still early afternoon, so we decided to go to Sav-La-Mar about thirty minutes away. Referred to as "Sav," the city is always hustling and bustling with people. If we wanted to girl watch, which we always did, sometimes we'd go there. It was away from the tourist spots and full of native people. On a previous trip, I had met a young lady named Stephanie and had been casually corresponding with her ever since. Hakeem and I had rented some motorcycles and were adventuring there one afternoon.

My booty radar detector had gone off when I saw Stephanie. "Keem check that out," as I pointed.

"Whoa, now dat's some booty!"

"No Negro, dat's a super booty!"

"I know dat's right, be right back."

Hakeem got the jump on me and pulled up to talk to the fine, young sexy.

Since all is fair in love and war, after he had gotten her attention, I pulled right in between them and explained, "I saw you first." It was on from then. It was obvious we were a tag team, having American accents and on motorcycles. The well spoken, pretty lady got a chuckle out of my interruption. Hakeem couldn't complain he would've used the same stunt on me. That had been the beginning of my correspondence with Stephanie.

I thought Stephanie was so fine, it didn't make sense. Sometimes I'd gaze at her from head to toe and just cringe. Throughout our subsequent conversations, Stephanie had mentioned that she sometimes lived with and assisted her Grandmother. Before this trip, their phone service had been cut off and I had no way of quickly letting her know that I would be in Jamaica.

"Since we're so close to Stephanie's house, why not stop by?" I suggested.

"It's all right with me," Hakeem replied.

"Of course," Freddy said. "You been trying to hit on her little sister."

"Don't hate!" Hakeem shot back.

"You old Chester-molester-ass rascal, you aughta be ashamed," Robbie added in his two cents.

We had already planned to hang out one more night at some beach party. I don't mind hanging with them but sometimes it's hard for four different minds to agree. If I was going to see Stephanie, this would be my last chance. A previous attempt earlier in the week had proved fruitless.

The road Stephanie's family lives on is narrow and full of potholes. It's hard to imagine that her family had moved their little two-bedroom hut to such a hard-to-reach to location. The truckers that move houses are some truck-driving experts. I know because I've seen them. We bounced down the lane and up to Stephanie's house. Three raggedy little mutts acting as guards surprised me as I got out of the car and approached the little house. To tell the truth, they got the better of me, which gave Hakeem fodder for later ribbing. The entire ruckus brought heads looking out windows, one of which was Stephanie's.

"Hello Gee," she yelled at the top of her lungs, "hang on, me soon come."

The house was the typical, primitive, wood-framed structure, sitting on concrete blocks. There was a gap between the ground and the bottom of the house which provided for the dogs, a hiding place. It needed painting years ago. I could hear scurrying, giggling, and whispering on the other side of the wall.

Stephanie's little sister, Lisa, is the sweetest little girl in the world. She is secured by her mother's continual presence. When I met Stephanie three years ago, Lisa was a terribly shy sixteen-year-old.

33

Gerald Randolph Howard

She may have weighed ninety pounds soaking wet, but she was adorably cute. I may have been the first black American that had befriended and interacted with the family. I felt it was always a unique occasion when I visited. Lisa had taken a liking to me and loved my visits. During my correspondence with Stephanie, Lisa had wanted to correspond with one of my friends also. She had written a letter to Hakeem and sent a picture. Hakeem's inconsiderate ass never even answered her. His disinterest always gave Lisa room to playfully chastise him.

Stephanie finally emerged to hellos, hugs, and introductions to everyone. Lisa close by, surprised me by her maturity and got her share of hugs also.

> "How long you been in Jamaica, Gee?" Stephanie's sweet voice melted my heart as she asked.
>
> "About six days."
>
> "Oh no, Me sorry you not able to get a hold of me. Me Mom said you come by. You know me have been staying wit me Grandma up in de hills. It's kinda hard to get messages right now."
>
> "Yeah I know. I hope everything is okay with her. You been doing okay?"

I love the calmness of Jamaicans, so relaxed. It's like they say, "no problem Mon." That, compounded by their accents, really gets to me. Stephanie is such a pretty, voluptuous young thing that a brotha couldn't help but want her.

I had never been intimate with her, but we have remained sweethearts/pen pals for the last three years or so. Every time I've come to this part of paradise, I would usually stop by. I'd get a joy out of going to the supermarket and hooking up dinner. What better authentic cooking could I get than straight from the native people? It's been nice too, developing our friendship and allowing it to take its natural course, rather than trying to take Stephanie straight to bed. I think that's why the family liked me. I was just easy going with them. Stephanie's father was usually off somewhere working so he was only around on an occasion or two. I'd always try to contribute to the house one way or another.

"Yes, me been doing ok, tank you. Me grandma is getting old and needs much care. Me try to help her as much as possible. But it's very hard sometimes, Gee. Me wish you here more often. Da money you give us helps a lot. You are a good mon, Gee."

"Well, how about joining us and getting something to eat? How's pizza sound?" I said gently, putting my arm around Lisa. "Lisa, you wanna go have some pizza with us?" I knew this invitation was irresistible because eating out was not something they could ordinarily afford. I also knew that Lisa was not going anywhere without her mom. Her mother knew the same.

Stephanie thought her mother and I were about the same age. I was at liberty to call her mom by her first name, Pat. Ordinarily, I wouldn't have done that, but she insisted. I do throw in a "yes or no, Ms Pat" when appropriate to show her respect.

"Pat, I know that Lisa is not going anywhere without you, so what do you think? Would you like to join us?"

Obviously, Pat started having children awfully young. As close as I could figure, Pat must have been about sixteen years old when Stephanie was born. So when I asked, the three family members acted just like giggly little girls. Pat said, "Okay, Gee dat be very nice."

There were already four of us in the car, and the ladies made seven. To them, it was nothing new to be so tightly packed in a car. To us, it was an exercise of creativity and planning how to get everyone in. After deciding who would sit where, whose arm would go around whom, and which person's lap to use, we were ready to ride.

"These damn potholes! My hemorrhoids need a break." Freddy declared.

"Freddy, who said you could talk? Excuse him, ladies, he's not used to being around people," I explained rather irately. That was always my biggest complaint about Freddy. The clown basically was a stone knucklehead and never knows what to say when.

"What him say?" Pat asked.

35

"He said he thinks the potholes might break our ride," Hakeem helped me out.

The potholes in the road were rough, but to the ladies it was nothing new. Smiling ear to ear, they all seemed just as happy as could be. I was happy to see them. The gang just hung on in.

We had good fun that evening and it was nice to see the ladies enjoying themselves. Finding beauty in simple things is an exercise I like to practice. After we finished our pizza, we milled around in the parking lot. Robbie, as usual, disappeared around a convenient corner to have his after breakfast, lunch or pizza joint. I brought out my camera to take some pictures. Stephanie was so picturesque. I took this opportunity to get some more shots of her. Lisa was her usual shy self. Freddy's Polaroid dispensed instant results that kept the ladies giddy.

"Ooh, ooh, I want this one!" Lisa shouted when she saw a good pose of herself.

Hakeem countered, "No, this is mine," snatching it from Lisa's hand. The chase was on. After a circle or two around the lot, Hakeem gave in. Freddy gave them all some shots I'm sure they took pride in.

We headed back through the potholes to the house and hung around outside. The dogs were in check now since their masters were there monitoring them. This was such a rare occasion; the girls welcomed our company.

I whispered to Stephanie, "You know I want you to go with me this evening."

"And you know I want to go, me been waiting for dis chance for a long time, Gee."

I could have melted right there, but Freddy interrupted, "Hey, no whispering allowed."

"Let me go in and tell Mom that me go wit you, me soon come," Stephanie whispered back in my ear. Lisa followed as if she were her shadow. It was starting to get dark. A few minutes passed and Stephanie called out from the house, "Gee, please come." I entered through the kitchen, which was very small. Pat motioned for me to

36

sit at the table as she sat also. Stephanie was in one of the other rooms, getting her things together.

Pat spoke with a bold Jamaican attitude, "Gee, me know you a long time and me trust you. Stephanie want to go wit you and it's okay wit me because me see dat look in her eye. You make her very happy. Dese girls all me have." She looked me dead in the eye, "Take care of me girl, you understand?"

This reminded me of the times I'd been lectured by the fathers of some of my teenage sweethearts. I thought this was kind of funny, because by now I knew all the correct things to say. Besides, I wasn't out to take advantage of Stephanie. She and I were really quite comfortable with each other. "Pat you know you don't have to worry when Stephanie is with me." We sat there probably five more minutes waiting for Stephanie. The conversation consisted primarily of me reassuring Pat that everything was going to be all right.

Stephanie had caught my attention the first day I met her. Her round booty shook beneath her sundress as if it were Jell-O. Her luscious looks made my mouth water.

When she came out ready to leave, she looked even more luscious. Mr. Johnson got hard. I can't be blamed for a man's perfectly natural reaction. I'm only human. As Stephanie said her goodbyes to Lisa and her mother, I tried to hide my instant excitement.

We headed out the door and the gang got all their goodbyes in. Stephanie and I found our corner in the back seat. Holding hands, I let her elbow rest on Johnson's head. Her smile let me know that she knew what was happening. She whispered in my ear, "I can't wait, either," as we headed back to the hotel.

The Peanut Gallery had already picked out the party spot on the beach. By the time we made the thirty-minute trip back, they were ready to get-on-wit-da-get-on. The evening with Pat, Stephanie, and Lisa hadn't been quite what they would have preferred to do. So they were all ready to let their savage beasts loose.

As we entered the hotel room, I laid Stephanie's bag on a chair.

"Let's sit outside Stephanie while the guys get

themselves together," I suggested.

"You friends are funny, Gee."

"Yes and they're always up to something goofy."

Our suite had a table setting on the porch and two single-person hammocks. We sat at the table and I pulled her chair as close to mine as possible.

"What would I rather be doing than sitting under the stars with you? Nothing. Where would I rather be then here? Nowhere. Who would I rather be with than you? No one."

"Gee, I feel da same way. Me been waiting for dis night. Me glad it's here. Me promise not to disappoint you. You be de mon of me dreams. Me hope you enjoy being wit me as much as me enjoy you."

"No, no, no, Steph, believe me I enjoy you a whole bunch more."

Stephanie kissed me as if she couldn't put her tongue far enough down my throat. And I took every inch of it, came up for air and did it again. Her hard nipples appeared like bright lights through her airy dress. I lightly pinched one.

This fine, sexy, little momma allowed me to do just exactly what I wanted to, and I appreciated the opportunity.

"Hey, hey, what's going on out here?" Robbie spoke softly as he headed toward the car.

"I'm falling in love, whatchu think?" I replied.

Stephanie giggled innocently as she looked dead in my eyes and said "Yup, me too."

On his way out, Hakeem said, "Yo, Gee, I'll yell atcha."

Freddy exited allowing the screen door to slam. "Bam!"

I shouted, "Freddy!"

"What?"

"You a buckethead."

"My bad."

I took Stephanie by the hand, walked inside, and locked and bolted the door. Neither of us had to say a word. We headed straight for the shower. She had no problems undressing herself. In fact, I think she was secretly putting on a show for me. She knew just what to do. I was first in the water and had a ringside seat. When her panties hit the floor, she looked at me as if to ask for my approval. The only thing I could say was "Girl... you know you fine."

"All for you, Gee."

Stephanie's body looked so smooth and soft. Those naturally firm breasts were every bit of thirty-eight inches. I think a man's infatuation with a woman's breast is related to a baby's contented suckling. Lord knows I like to suck some. By this time, Mr. Johnson was playing Army Sergeant and standing at full attention. I enjoyed watching Stephanie watching him. She stepped over the edge of the tub and everything fell right in place. She was the perfect size for me; a couple of inches shorter and about 140 pounds, just juicy for no reason. How could a brotha not appreciate this? I thought, "it doesn't get any better then this, Gee. You better enjoy this while you have the chance." Warm soapy water was getting everywhere, wet kisses were wetter. Our two sets of hand couldn't touch enough places and Sgt. Johnson was just being a big show-off. I had my back to the showerhead and backed underneath between the falling water and the wall. I reached around the curtain for the condoms I had strategically placed in my toiletry bag. By the time Sarg was fully clothed in his rain gear, Stephanie's foot was resting on the edge of the tub. Everybody knew what to do. Sgt. Johnson knew where to go and Stephanie knew where to lead him. I turned the water off, grabbed everybody, took three steps, and sat us on the vanity. With both hands free, I covered Stephanie's back to absorb some of the water, turned and took a few more steps, and gently laid her on my bed. Sgt. Johnson and I were very content to say the least. I assume Stephanie was also by the quiet moaning sounds that were music to my ears.

"Girl... We're singing in perfect three-part harmony." I said as my buddy and I performed in perfect pitch. We never missed a note. By the time the evening was over, we received two standing ovations.

The Three Stooges were either considerate or Stephanie and I were just exhausted by our evening's command performances.

The sun coming in the bedroom window woke me first. I got up to use the bathroom and came back to see Stephanie awakening. "Good morning, beautiful," I whispered.

"Good morning, handsome."

"Girl..."

"Boy...."

"I know that's right. Would you like your breakfast here or on the porch? I can have it ready in ten minutes."

"Me come outside."

"Cool."

As usual, the smell of whatever I was cooking awoke the Peanut Gallery. I was just hoping that they hadn't dragged in whomever from the night before. Robbie was the first to appear.

"Is it ready yet?"

"Is what ready yet?" I replied, as if I was "supposed" to be somebody's cook.

"I know I have to do the dishes."

"Yup, you know the routine Cuz."

Stephanie appeared with a morning housecoat on that showed boobs bouncing everywhere.

"And don't be looking at my baby, either." I whispered to Robbie.

"Damn, Bro...too late."

"Two eggs sunny side up, turkey bacon and toast Grant Howell style, is that okay, baby?"

"Tank you Gee, me tink me gonna keep you here wit me."

"I have coffee and orange juice, sweetheart, which would you like?"

"Can me have both?"

"Baby, you can have anything your heart desires."

"How about some more t'ree-part harmony?"

"If I didn't have this plane to catch, girl, we could start singing right now."

Stephanie aggressively ate the breakfast I prepared and even picked a banana from the bunch hanging from a beam overhead.

The telephone rang. "Yo, Gee, it's for you,"Freddy yelled from behind his door.

> "Telephone?" I wondered who in the world could be calling me. It could be the hotel management since today was our checkout day. I grabbed the closest line, which was just inside the door.
>
> "Yo, this is Gee."
>
> "Good morning, sir, how are you today." The familiar female voice replied.

What an inconvenient time to call, especially since Stephanie was within earshot. To appear as though this was no one special, I kept talking. There was no noise, music, or anything else in the room to drown out my conversation.

> "Hey, Jacy, how did you get this number?" Stephanie's attention was on my conversation. Obviously, Robbie put two and two together when he heard me say Jacy's name, and struck up a conversation with Stephanie.

Jacy avoided the question and replied, "Fine tank you. I guess that you and your friends are getting ready to leave us?"

> "This is an unexpected surprise, but yes, all good things come to an end."
>
> "Dat sounds like someone famous say dat."
>
> "Yes, me."
>
> "You get de chance to do everyting you wanted to do?"
>
> "No, but I'm sure I'll be back to get another chance. What leads you to bless me with such a surprise this morning?"

"Don't tell anyone but me like your bald head."

"I knew it. I could see it in your eyes. You're like all the rest. I wish someone would appreciate me for my intellect." I spoke in a quiet voice. With Robbie's help, it appeared that Stephanie didn't know I was talking to another female.

"Yup, Me have to confess. Me wanted to rub it de first day Me see you."

"You could have."

"Well how bout de next time?"

"I don't know when that will be, but if you can wait, that's fine with me."

"Well, Gee, I know you busy to catch yo plane..."

I interrupted. "No, I'm not too busy. I appreciate your call."

I noticed that Robbie was running out of food and conversation with Stephanie. "But before you hang up, give me your number and I'll yell atcha to let you know we made it home safely."

"Gee, you no need dat as an excuse to have me number. Me wanted you to have it anyway."

"Cool, let me go get something to write with." I laid the phone down and left the room. "All right go ahead."

"8-7-6 is me area code and de number is 9-5-5-7-7-1-0." I didn't want to disregard Stephanie, so I needed to hurry up and end this conversation.

"Well, Miss Jacy Weber, you made my day."

"And you made mine, Gee Howell."

"Take care and we'll talk again, okay?"

"Okay."

The entire Peanut Gallery was up now. Hakeem was in the bathroom, Freddy was in the kitchen and Robbie had disappeared again. I assumed he was going to get his usual after meal hit of reefer.

"Fellas, we got to hit the airport by one. I'm gonna run

Stephanie home real quick and I'll be right back."

Hakeem shouted from the bathroom, "Yo, Gee, you want me to ride witcha?"

"No, Hakeem. Lisa doesn't want to see you today." I knew the real motive behind his inquiry.

"Bye, Stephanie, see you next time. Tell Mom and Lisa I said 'bye.'" Hakeem continued to shout.

"Okay, Hakeem, me tell dem for you, take care."

Stephanie and I arrive at her house to see Pat washing clothes by hand. Lisa was hanging clothes on a line that stretched from a tree to a nail at the corner of the house. The patchy, grassed backyard was their laundry room. As Pat would finish the scrubbing in one washtub, they'd go to another to rinse. This was not the first time I had seen their method.

"Ladies, ladies, ladies, you are working too hard." I said, as I kissed Pat on the forehead and hugged her neck.

Lisa ran to me and gave me a big hug, "Hey, Gee, what's up?"

"Where you get that from? Asking me "what's up," like you grown? I'm sad and glad. That's what's up."

"What you mean?" Lisa inquired.

"I'm sad because I have to catch a plane at noon and I can't take you with me. I'm glad to be getting away from those little monster attack dogs you got." Stephanie started laughing.

"No, Mon, dey like you, Gee." Lisa replied playfully.

"Yeah, they'd like me for their dinner."

"Gee, you a good Mon, you always welcome here." Pat squinted from the sunlight as she looked up at me, her hands still scrubbing away. I could see hard times in her face. I doubt that she had ever been to a hair salon to be pampered or fussed over. These were good, honest, lovely people and I really appreciated them. I wish that I could've done more for them. Whatever they had, I was always welcome to, even though I only showed my face once or twice a year. Stephanie took me by the hand and led me into the kitchen.

"Gee, when you coming back?" She gave me a full body hug as she looked me lovingly in the eyes.

"Tomorrow?" I joked.

"No, mon for real when you coming back?"

"Pretty girl, you know I never really know. I just come when my business allows me."

"Well, at least promise me dat you'll come to see me whenever you come."

"You know that's an easy promise to keep. I promise. I promise. I promise."

"Oh and dere's someting else me want you to promise."

"Okay," I replied.

"No more singing t'ree-part harmony till you get back."

I looked at her with surprise and chuckled, "Okay I pro, pro, pro..." Stephanie tightened her bear hug trying to cut off my breath.

I yelled outside towards Lisa, "Lisa help! A monster is attacking me again." Stephanie stifled my yelling with a sweet goodbye-kiss. I savored her luscious lips. I know she felt Mr. Johnson getting hard because she pulled me closer.

"All right, you know I got a plane to catch, don't get started." She kissed me again. "Bye Pat. Bye Lisa. See you next time."

"Goodbye, Gee," they said in unison. I dropped some grocery money on the kitchen table as I went out the front. Stephanie watched as I drove away, still waving until I was out of sight.

Back to the ATL

Chapter 5

The flight back to Atlanta was routine. Check bags in, go through customs, and the same old routine requiring patience to ensure that all is well. Why do I always have to sit right next to the folks who snore? I must have been really tired because I did catch up on a little sleep. A nap kind of makes the chore of the trip back seem a little less time-consuming.

It's true that there's no place like home. When I return home after an extended period away, I feel like I have to put everything away immediately so I can feel like I'm home and ready to proceed with my regular routine. After watering my plants, I'll make it to the grocery store because I just have to have milk and bread. All the Captain Crunch and Fruit Loops in the world are no good without milk. Sometimes I forget to change my answering service from saying when I'll be back and please call again. Usually a friend will remind me of that a day or two later. Yeah, I still have a bad memory.

The phone is usually a quick reminder that I run a business out of my home and I'm back to reality. So I've learned to grin and bear it, answer it, be nice, which is kind of hard to do sometimes. Imagine someone calling at midnight to inquire about moving rates. It took me a while to learn to politely say, "I'll be in my office in the morning at nine; do you mind calling me then?" I've gotten it down pretty good now. Anything that you do over and over again, you get better at, you know. That means dealing with customers and employees and a whole bunch of ass-kicking hard work. Oh, slinging furniture isn't fun. Complaining just makes things harder, so I try to be positive, diligent, and persevering until my next idea for another adventure arises.

The reward for working so hard can be financially beneficial. I appreciate all the rewards that come with that. I appreciate the Lord blessing me with the strength and determination to be able to do it.

My excitement is in being creative and adventurous. I'm glad that I make the bucks to have my getaways. I like being challenged. Being raised in a household of only boys created competitive spirits. We always challenged each other and to win meant that you had to come up with something the others couldn't or wouldn't do. That environment left me with a yearning to go all the way out to the edge. Live life to the fullest. There have been times that I may have gotten too close to the limit and had to pay the price of overstepping my boundaries. To go to the edge, look over, and come back to safety is thrilling. Besides, who wants to live a dull, ho-hum life? Shoot, as far as we know we only live once. So, like I always say "if you don't do what you wanna do, it ain't nobody's fault but your own." Years ago, I tested my nerve and jumped out of an airplane. I even took thirty days once and rode my motorcycle completely around the U.S. Even Teddy Pendergrass sang it - "life is a song worth singing, so sing it." Personally, I don't want to leave any stone unturned or opportunity untested. When it's all over and done with, I want to be able to know that I did what I wanted. But until then, I got some furniture to sling so I can make these duckies.

Gettin' Deeper

Chapter 6

O ver the three years that I have known Jacy, I have come to feel like part of the family. Our friendship has prospered over that which I had with Stephanie. Stephanie was fine as all outdoors but I knew she was too young. Besides, I learned that she had gotten pregnant and had a baby, which took me out of the picture anyway. Jacy and I have gotten quite close. I'm always welcome to stay as long as I'd like. On the occasions that I do stay, the money that I ordinarily would spend on hotel rooms I donate to the house, either in groceries or cash. Why be a freeloader? I'm glad to contribute because I know the house could use the money. If I leave a couple of hundred bucks, it makes me feel good. I get great authentic Jamaican food and a chance to be with my sweetheart for a week. I imagine I've spent a small fortune in calling cards keeping in contact and have written an untold number of letters. It's all good, I recognize that's the price you have to pay for being in a long-distance relationship.

Jacy is thirty years old now. Even though she takes care of her niece, she has had no children. So after three years, she is wanting the thing that all young ladies want from a long-term relationship - commitment. Yup, that's the word that a single man with a grown daughter hates to hear - commitment.

Besides, at forty-nine I have reached the point in my life that I'm still in good physical condition, and more financially secure than I have ever been. Why change anything now? I'm on a roll. I remember my Grandfather being single most of his life. He got married again at fifty and said that he figured he'd do it before he got too old to offer a woman anything. That made sense, so somewhere along the way I figured fifty-five would be a good number for me.

There's a world-famous restaurant and hangout in Jamaica called

Rick's Cafe. The primary attraction is that it offers the most picturesque sunset you'd ever want to see. People come from miles around to socialize, eat and relax in the aura of the atmosphere.

Native Jamaicans entertain and hustle tourists with dives and jumps off the cliffs into the ocean. The most daring and experienced jump from the trees above the forty-foot cliffs. Occasionally, you might see a visitor who obviously has some high diving experience put in a show also. This has come to be a hangout for Jacy and me when I'm there. She ordinarily won't go. So when I'm there, we splurge and "do what the rich folks do." There is always live music, so we can dance if we want, have something refreshing to quench our thirst or throw down on a full course meal. Jacy, being rather shy, virtually never dances there, thinks the food is much too expensive, but will have some rum punch.

"Gee, what you doing?" I remember her asking.

"What you mean, what am I doing?" As I begin disrobing down to my swim trunks.

"Oh no, not again. You know me hate when you do dis to me."

"Do what? What you talking 'bout, girl. I'm just going to cool down a bit. You know how hot I get when I'm around you. Besides, why don't you join me?" I ask knowing darn well she is not about to dive off anything. Jacy is a good swimmer but diving is another story.

"I'm not going to watch, me hate when you do dis." She complains.

"Whatever."

Standing thirty-five feet above the ocean looking down at the water gives me a thrill. It's like going across a bridge looking down and imagining what it would be like to jump off. Of the many times that I've been to Rick's, I have seen people who have had too much to drink, get pumped up by either their friends or reefer, or both, and should sit their asses down, but machismo kicks in and they have to test their nerve. Some do okay and some don't. The native divers who hustle the tourists, chaperone the place and act as lifeguards. I remember one time the emergency crew had to come. This poor fellow couldn't decide if he wanted to dive or jump and hit the water with his body positioned somewhere in between. Bam! The crowd usually trips out. Of course, since Rick's is a big money maker for the tourist industry, they get emergency care immediately. I've found that the best way to approach the cliffs is not to stand there thinking about it too long; just go. After you commit, it's too late to turn back then, nerve or not. To tell the truth, my technique isn't quite good enough for it not to hurt somewhere. The last time I dove off the cliffs at Rick's my brother's mouth overloaded his booty, and our bet cost him twenty bucks.

Work, Work, Work

Chapter 7

A previous customer with a three-bedroom house coming from Miami was scheduled for the week coming. The operating authority that I have doesn't allow me to transport out of the state. However, every now and then, a previous customer or a friend of a friend might ask me to do something long distance. To tell the truth, I've been trucking long enough to know what I can and can't get away with. If I use a U-Haul or an unmarked truck, the inspectors won't know that I'm going outside my jurisdiction. I hate not being able to do out-of-state moves because they're easy big money. I usually ask the guys who work for me if any of them would be interested in making a trip. It just so happened this time that Chuck Dailey, whom we call "Big Chuck," would be the only crew supervisor available.

I once saw Chuck carry a sleeper sofa up a flight of stairs by himself. A sofa can be heavy sometimes, but one with a mattress and a steel frame in it is nothing to play with. After that, he had my respect as a genuine tough guy; everyone has called him "Big Chuck" since then. On one occasion, Robbie and Big Chuck worked together, which resulted in them falling out. One of my many complaints about Robbie is that he is a slow worker. The other complaints are personal and have nothing to do with work; I still can't understand why a thirty-something year old man would still live with his mother. He's clean-cut, careful, and never damages furniture, but if for some reason you need to hurry, Robbie is not the one you want. Big Chuck had to be in court around three one afternoon. He called in saying that Robbie was dragging booty and he wasn't going to make it. I drove to the job and relieved him in time to make his appointment. Since then, Chuck will not work with Robbie. I have spoken to Robbie time and time again about being more enthusiastic and energetic, but to no avail. Unfortunately, there are disadvantages to hiring relatives. When Robbie came to me and requested that I allow him to make the trip, I thought it rather odd.

"Oh, so you and Big Chuck have kissed and made up?" I asked.

"What you mean?" Robbie played dumb.

"What do you mean what do I mean? You know darn well I try to keep you and Big Chuck off the same truck," I spoke with authority.

"I got no problem working with him as long as he lets me work at my own pace." Robbie replied.

"No, I disagree, Robbie. Sometimes you got to get-on wit da get-on. You know what it is. When the customer sees you hustling, they don't mind giving up them tips, Bro. You know Big Chuck's sofa bed carrying tail knows how to get his," I explained.

"And you know I make mine by being careful and not tearing up any furniture. That's what I'm talking about, being careful."

"Robbie, there's a big difference between being careful and being slow. You and I have been through this before."

"Besides, I figure we could stay at Aunt Quinn's house and save on a hotel room. You know she don't mind. I haven't seen her in ages." Robbie was pleading now.

"All right, Robbie, don't start singing the blues. You talk to Big Chuck about it and if it's okay with him then it's okay with me. Get it together quickly because the trip leaves next Wednesday."

To me, work is work. Work is something you have to do to make money. The Bible says if you don't work, you don't eat. To be honest, I don't know where that exact verse is located, but it's in there. "Working by the sweat of your brow," was the punishment heaped on Adam and Eve for being disobedient in the Garden of Eden. How dare I think that hard work is going to elude me? That bit of knowledge and wisdom has helped me tolerate doing what I have to do. I do it also because this is how I know to make the most money that I can. Moving furniture has never been fun or easy. I do get some satisfaction knowing that I have the gut determination to do something that other men won't. When people say, "I don't see how you guys do this everyday," I just smile and tell them "only the strong survive," and keep on pushing.

If work is work, then what else do we do? Sometimes we are introduced to others by our occupational titles. Thus, we are defined by what we do for a living. "This is John Doe and he is a fireman. I'd like for you to meet Ms. So-n-so Johnson and she is the CEO of her own bank." I declare that I am more than my occupation and proceed to talk about some of the things I do other than work. Life is a blessing and a celebration. Every day can be Christmas or a birthday. If I don't do what I want to do with my life, it's no one's fault but mine. I sure would hate to get to the end and ponder about what should've, would've or could've been. I don't want to leave any stone unturned, opportunity missed, or adventure not taken. Unfortunately resources only allow us to do so much. Another motto; "This is my life and I'm going to enjoy it." So I'm turning over stones, taking every opportunity and adventure. I can't wait till the next one.

A day after Robbie was to have spoken to Big Chuck, I had the weekly schedule already planned.

Standing in the middle of my parking lot is not the best place to transact business, but my cell phone allows me not to miss any calls.

"Yo, boss man, can I yell at you?" Big Chuck interrupted me as I was scheduling another appointment. He just demonstrated another reason why I appreciate getaways; customers and watermelon-headed employees. I held up one finger telling him I'd be right there.

"Oh, you didn't see me on the phone?" I asked.

"My bad, boss, but I'm mad at you."

"You can be mad, but you don't have to interrupt me on the phone. What... What'chu want?"

"I want you to loan me one of your motorcycles, I got a hot date tonight. I'm trying to perpetrate like I got it going

52

on."

"All right, which one you want, the chopper or Ducati?"

"Man you ought to quit. You'd rather let me ride one of your girlfriends than let me take one of your bikes."

"Oh, Big Chuck, you aught to be ashamed of yourself," I responded in a nerdy voice. "How can I be of assistance to you today, sir?"

"You do that too well, I knew you were a white boy in your previous life. I checked out the schedule for the week and I see you got me and Slow-motion heading to the ocean. What's up with that?"

"Robbie just left to do a two-bedroom apartment, I told him to get it straight with you about going to Miami. He didn't say anything to you about it?"

"Nope." Chuck looked at me disgustedly. "And this is a three-bedroom, boss, you know I'm gonna need some decent help."

I paused and thought for ten seconds. "Okay, Chuck, check this out, let's do it this way. I remember this customer because I moved him down there. I stayed at his crib that night and he greased my palm real well. He's very generous; at least he was back then. When he pays the bill, if he gives you anything extra, it's all yours. How's that?"

"Gee, you know there is never any guarantee that a customer will tip."

"I know that's right Chuck, but if he does... okay, I tell you what. I'll call a local U-Haul center and arrange to have you two more men to help load. That'll make up for slow-motion."

"All right, boss, you da man.

"No Chucky Cheese, you da man. I'mma put my foot in Robbie's butt. I know damn well I told him to yell at you about this." Chuck's willingness to grin and bear it made up for his rude interruption of my phone call.

"No problem, boss, I'll take care of this, but I still want

to ride one of your bikes. You can keep your sweethearts 'cause I got my own." Chuck replied as he headed to his morning appointment.

A disadvantage of operating a home-based business like mine is that I have things that I can't keep at the house, such as trucks and employees. I meet my men daily at a parking lot that I rent from a storeowner. He is happy to lease out the space that would ordinarily not be used, and having large trucks, I need a good bit of room. So our arrangement works out well for both of us. My days usually start by meeting my men there and giving them their assignments. The disadvantage at times is that I have to stop what I might be doing throughout my day to meet them there to address whatever dilemma might arise. Sometimes I have to meet them to collect the day's revenue, especially if I don't feel comfortable trusting that particular crew leader until I see them the next morning. Words of wisdom that I have gathered from older men is "count your own money, son." My addition to that, now that I'm getting to be that same old man is, "You can't trust just anyone with your money, son." Unfortunately, it took me a few learning experiences for me to grasp that lesson. The men that I have working with me right now have been with me long enough to be trustworthy.

I needed to talk to Robbie, so I thought I'd kill two birds with one stone. I met the crew to collect the revenue and share with him what was on my mind. "Yo, fellas, everybody all right?" I called as they exited the truck. "Is the back door of the truck locked?"

Robbie replied. "Yeah, I got it." All the supplemental duties —securing, cleaning, verifying directions, are the duties of the helpers. I want the drivers to concentrate on customer relations and driving safety. I figure a driver should never have to sweep out the truck, and a helper doesn't need to know what a customer was charged. Unfortunately, Robbie, after five years, doesn't have the ambition to be anything more than be a helper. That's probably why he's in his thirties and still living with his mother. Yes, they write songs about guys like him. TLC, the female singing group from Atlanta sings about not needing a scrub;

"If you don't have a car and you're walking,

Oh yes son I'm talking about you.

Risking Paradise

If you live at home with your momma

Oh yes son I'm talking about you."

That's one of my pet peeves about Robbie. He just doesn't have any drive or ambition. Sometimes I have to ask him, "What are you thinking about?" I tried to spark some kind of fire in him. I've finally come to the realization that you have to let people be the way they want to be. It's not my responsibility to motivate and inspire someone who doesn't want to be motivated or inspired. I do when I can, but some people aren't reachable. Some people are just going to be slackers. Yeah, that's right, I said it, "slack."

I took the day's revenue and looked at the contracts to verify that all the numbers and information were correct. "See you guys tomorrow, same place, same time. Have a good day."

"All right, boss" came from the three-man group almost in unison.

"Yo, Robbie," I got his attention as we headed to leave.

"Yeah, Gee, what's up?" He replied.

"You tell me what's up."

"Trying to make a dollar out of fifteen cents."

"I'm trying to make "cents" out of why you didn't say anything to Big Chuck about going with him down to Miami."

"I'm trying to figure out what you wanted me to say to him."

"All right, Robbie, work with me here. You could have mentioned that there was a trip coming up to Miami that you wanted to go on."

"Yeah."

"You could have mentioned that staying with your Aunt Quinn gave you a motivating interest to go."

"Yeah."

"You could have mentioned you wanted to show him that y'all can still work together. Come on Robbie don't be so shortsighted, you're not the only person I'm trying to watch out for, keep duckies in yo pocket."

"Yeah," he whispered.

"Not only that, you and I both know I told you to say something to Big Chuck about it."

"Yeah."

"Now just give me one legitimate reason why you didn't do like I asked. Oh, I don't pay you exactly when I say I will? Oh, I don't have all your money when I'm supposed to?"

"Why you gotta go there?"

"Damn, Robbie, this is a two-way street, you know. The world doesn't spin just for you. Sometimes y'all make me wanna spit."

"Okay, okay, calm down. I didn't think it was all that important, Gee."

"Like I ain't got other stuff to take care of, Brotha, what's the matter witchu? I'll tell you what, if Big Chuck don't hear anything encouraging from you real quick, I'll go my damn self and you can just take those few days off."

Everybody knows that I have a thousand other things to do. They also know me well enough that when I say," I'll do something my damn self," I'm getting ready to blow. The ghetto was starting to come out of me as I realized that losing my temper is the exact thing that I try to steer away from with these guys. Pausing for a second to take a breath, I concluded it wasn't anything new, or even worth the frustration.

"Okay, okay, I got you, boss." Robbie replied in an apologetic voice. "I got this. I'll get straight with Big Chuck, promise."

"The trip is Wednesday." I reminded.

"I got you, boss."

"Now I'm done with this."

"I got you, boss."

"Y'all burn my high yellow bootyhole sometimes," I said

56

under my breath but loud enough for Robbie to hear.

"Huh?"

"I said I hope you have a good evening," I jumped on my motorcycle and declared my workday over.

I rode home to switch bikes. My infatuation with powerful machines is manifested in my love for motorcycling. To have so much control at my fingertips is exhilarating. I've even slept on one of them. While circling the U.S. I'd get so sleepy after traveling hours on end that occasionally, I'd have to stop just to close my eyes for a minute. I'd place the Goldwing on the center stand and stretch my feet towards the handle bars and lay backwards. I'd cover myself with a jacket concealing my friends Smith and Wesson, and I was straight. I was never bothered, but when sleep hits you like that it's too dangerous to try to keep going. One of the regular Monday night motorcycle hangouts spots is The Vortex, in an area called "Little Five Points." All the free spirits hang out there. Someone might be playing their guitar hustling a few bucks; others might have a bite to eat in the open-air food courts on the avenue. The crowd is racially mixed as opposed to the Paradise on Sundays where the bikers are usually all black. The Brothas sport the crotch rockets but the white boys have the interesting stuff. Bikes that you don't ordinarily see. You might see anything from a Boss Hoss with a 350 c.i. engine, to an original Indian restored to showroom condition. When I get around guys who appreciate creativity, I like to bring my chopper. We admire each other's ideas and discuss shop. I spent a couple of years chopping a 1975 Honda 750; it ended up being very different from stock. So I appreciate when people check me out, too. It always interests the older guys who think it looks familiar, and are spellbound when I verify that it is what they think it is.

I milled around for an hour or so, saw a couple of familiar faces, nice bikes, and when I figured that I had enough, I headed home. The summer evening air is the best time of year to ride. One of my biggest joys is riding my motorcycles.

Tuesday afternoon I get a call from Big Chuck. "Yo, boss."

"Hello, may I help you?" I answered in my standard professional voice.

"It's Chuck, I got a problem. Our customer's new house is

not ready. The builder is standing right here talking about all the rain and humidity hasn't allowed the varnished floors to dry properly. He said he needs another twenty-four hours."

"Chuck," I sighed. "I don't need this right now. Heck, the rain didn't stop us from getting the furniture over there."

"I hear ya, boss, but I do see that the floors are still sticky."

"You did mention to the customer that this was not in the plan?"

"Yup, sure did."

A few seconds of silence goes by as Chuck and I try to figure out how to solve this dilemma.

"You know that I got you and that truck planned to go out of town tomorrow morning?"

"Yup, sure do."

"As a matter of fact, I got a two-bedroom apartment today that wants to go to Valdosta ASAP. They said tomorrow morning would be fine with them."

"That would make the Miami trip even more worthwhile, boss man."

"Yup, sure would. All right, you guys think about this for a minute and try to figure out some kind of solution. If you put the furniture in the garage, it would be all right with me."

"No garage, boss."

"Darn... Okay Chuck let me call you back in a minute."

"Later boss."

These kinds of changes happen every now and then. The challenge now is to figure out how to solve the problem and still keep everybody happy. Big Chuck's customer surely knows that I'm gonna charge them extra for this unforeseen roadblock. So I have no problem, really, with that truck being tied up with furniture all night. I just have to deal with needing an empty truck immediately. I called Hakeem.

"Yo, Keem."

"Yo, Gee."

"What's up?"

"What's up?"

"All right, don't start playing, I need you to help me figure out something."

"I'm not playing, what's up?"

"Where are you?"

"Man, that job you sent us on was a whiz. The customer had gotten all the little stuff out of the house. It only took us three hours to finish. I got some beef lined up already and I'm heading in."

"Oh, so your crew is done?" I inquired.

"Yes, sir."

"Well, check this out. Big Chuck can't unload his truck today because of some wet floors and I was planning for him to head out of town tomorrow."

"Damn, Gee, sounds like you got a pretty big problem."

"I don't need you to throw salt on my wound Hakeem. I need for you too come through big time for us."

"'Us' don't have a problem, boss. It sounds like 'you' got a problem."

"Oh, which young lady are you hooking up with Hak, the one I fixed you up with at the Essence Festival or the one I hooked you up with at Vegas Nights? You know you still owe me, soul-brotha-number-one. I been wondering and wondering just when you gonna pay me back."

"Okay, Gee, what you need me to do?"

"That's what I thought you'd say. I need for you to take Big Chuck's job to Florida tomorrow."

"What? Damn."

"As a matter of fact, I need for you to tow your storage trailer behind my dually. I got a two-bedroom that needs to be picked tonight, if possible, to go to Valdosta. Drop it off, then head down to Miami and bring back a three-bedroom. I can take the Isuzu tomorrow and do the jobs that I had scheduled for you to do. That chick I introduced you to from Vegas Nights sure is fine, you still see her, don't you?"

"Gee, you done bumped yo head. I know my trailer is big, but it's not going to take a three-bedroom.

"I already got that taken care of. I got U-Haul sending out some help. I'll just tell them to bring out about a twenty-footer that can pull the trailer. Robbie can drive the dually back. Oh, and the Lady I hooked you up with at the Essence Festival is gorgeous, isn't she? She spoiled your booty at the Peachtree Plaza last weekend didn't she?"

"Well, today is your lucky day, Gee. The beef I was supposed to hook up with ain't either one of those two ladies. If she were, you'd be doo-doo out of luck brotha, and that's the truth.

"Hakeem, you my number one colored boy, you know that?"

"Colored boy?"

"Yeah, I didn't want to say 'nigga,' you know I'm trying to take that word out of my vocabulary."

"Just remember that I'm your 'number one colored boy' when you pay me."

My silly impromptu song showed Hakeem my appreciation for saving the day;

"I got you, Keem.

I got you Keem.

I got you Kee-ee-ee-ee,

Kee-ee-ee-ee Keem."

"Gee?"

"What?" I answered and fell right into his trap.

"You stupid... bye."

I called Chuck immediately. "Big Chuck, I got everything straight. Tell the customer the fee for coming out again is an additional hour and overnight storage is fifty dollars."

"You know I know the routine, boss."

"So that's the scoop, Chuck, write them up and head on in."

"Oh by the way boss man, does this mean that I don't have to deal with slow-motion for the next few days?"

"Have a good day, Chuck."

"I must be living right, boss."

"I guess so Chuck. Later, bro."

Dear Lover

Chapter 8

It's ten o'clock. I made it through another one. Lawdy, Lawdy, Lawdy. I can't count how many times I have said that easing into my steamy hot Jacuzzi. I appreciate the peace and solitude, the comfort and serenity of making it though another day; having withstood whatever challenges just to make a buck. There's no use complaining because this is what I chose to do, keeping in mind that only the strong survive. I received a letter from Jacy today. Reading it at the end of the day takes me further into peacefulness and serenity.

Dear Lover,

Man has not created the words to describe the love I have for you inside. To say the least I miss you, but for me to accurately describe how I long for you is like:

a day without sunshine,

a grape without a vine,

a future without time,

or rhythm without rhyme.

I received your letter today and again I have wind on which to soar. I saw a heavenly aura about the postman as he delivered it. It came right on time; Jah is never late. Obviously you have not forgotten about me as you go about you daily routine. Your comforting words soothe me as a pacifier does an infant. I know that life there is more exciting than the boring life I have here. Fortunately I have my books to take my mind away, my imagination to keep me close to you. I know that I'm not as fortunate as all those American women I see on television. I sometimes wonder why you might be interested in such a simple person, when a man like you could have any woman. You erect my posture when you mention beauty in life's simple things. You strengthen my stride. Being your permanent partner would be a dream come true, yet time goes on. What direction is my life going? You know that I have had my eyes only on you. You know that I am not interested in any others but you. You know that all I want is you. If I had the money to waste on wine, how could it be as sweet as when your tongue touches mine? You are the first and last earthly thing that I think about every day. I look forward so much to your phone calls and your letters. My mind wonders when I call and you are not at home. I know that you probably have other girlfriends but I don't care. All I want is to be your wife. I know that I can keep you happy. I know I can be a good wife to you, Mr. Howell. The lottery should give such a chance. I'm sorry to keep repeating myself. Could this have been my dream since I laid eyes on your bald head?

So what if you are older than I am.

All I want is to be with you.

So what if you are not interested in having more children.

All I want is to be with you.

Gee, make me the happiest woman in the world. You don't have to wait until you are fifty-five. Why not get this life started now? You are the love of my life. I miss you and can't wait to see you again. Last night after you called I felt as if we had never been apart. I fell asleep dreaming of your head on my stomach. Orgasmic strokes of your baldness, awoke me only to try to go back to sleep and revisit my dream. I look forward to the next time when you are in my bed and I can watch you sleep. You are just like a baby, my big baby. I will close now for fear of boring you. You are the sunshine of my life. I impatiently wait...

Love Jacy.

Another Day, Another Dollar

Chapter 9

It's Wednesday morning. I have to physically work with one of the crews today. Big Chuck is tied up delivering his holdover load, Freddy has gotten his crew going, and I call Hakeem.

"Good morning, sir."

"Eh," he replied.

"What? Let's try that again, young man. Good morning," I repeated with even more energy in my voice.

"What, Gee, what you want?"

"Boy, I'll slap you through this telephone! I've told you about being so lackadaisical."

"I'm not being lacka...lacka. Whatever you said, I just got work to do."

"Well, either you can go about it with energy, or you can accept it as burdensome."

"Good morning, Gee, how are you today? Isn't it a wonderful day today?" Hakeem acted excited.

"Now dat's what I'm talking bout. Run it down to me, what's the scoop?"

"You know your cousin sure is slow."

"He's *your* brother."

"We just finished loading up. The customer didn't mind helping, he said he was ready to get up and out'a here."

"That's good. I'm out here slaving, too, so keep your cell

on and I'll yell at you periodically. Cool?"

"Cool."

Hakeem, being my right hand man, knows what it is to sometimes have to grin and bear it. I appreciated him coming through for me at the last minute. He has worked for me off and on since he was thirteen years old. He used to tell me about going to junior high school with a wad of cash. Hakeem makes more than any of the others and has more responsibilities. He knows, being my cousin and the son I never had, the plan is for him to eventually run the business. He sees the money I make and the potential benefits.

As the day progressed, I gave Hakeem a call. "Yo, Hakeem, dis Gee."

"Yo, man, what's happening?"

"Just calling to see how you're doing." The reception was bad on his cell.

"I can barely hear you, but I'm in Valdosta, just finished unloading."

"Wow you been rolling, man." I shouted to compensate for the bad reception.

"Yeah, well you know having the trailer I don't have to stop at the weigh stations, and like I said the customer didn't mind helping."

"No problems or damages?"

"Nope, in fact he gave me an extra honey-hun for being on the ball."

"Good, there was room for him to do that. I gave him a discounted price just to get the job. I figured making something was better than making nothing since we were going that way. Besides, we gave the guy one-day service on a one-day notice. He should have helped and given you guys a little extra. Keep eighty bucks for coming through for me and give Robbie twenty. I'll probably..." The cell phone went dead.

It's Friday morning, and I get a call from Hakeem.

"Yo, Gee."

"Good morning, sir," I replied.

"We're at the customer's house loading up. I remember this guy. I helped you move him down here."

"Oh, okay, to tell the truth, I don't remember who helped me."

"Yes you do, that was the time we stopped on the way back and went fishing. The time we saw those Mexican guys trying to catch that alligator. You remember."

"Okay, yeah, I remember, my bad."

"Check this out. He has gotten rid of a lot of stuff. He said he had a yard sale and just didn't want to keep hauling all that stuff around."

"Okay," I replied.

"It looks like I'll be able to get everything on the trailer easily. So when these cats from U-Haul split, I'll let them take this truck back and we can save them duckies."

"Boy, you all right, you my number one colored boy. Let's do this; if he's got about half the stuff that I anticipated, I don't want to take advantage of him on the bill. You know what I mean?"

"Yeah, Gee, I feel ya, but you know he's got money, plus he bought extra insurance."

"Okay then tell him we're not going to charge him for the extra insurance and take off another three hundred. Shoot, we're getting four-grand out of half a load. I can let him slide a little on the bill."

"Yeah, that makes sense. So we got here last night and stayed at Quinn's. I guess we'll stay one more night and head back to the ATL tomorrow. You know I got to get Uncle Willie out of the house before we head back."

"Sounds like a plan to me."

"I'm using the customer's phone right now cause my battery died on mine. I don't have my charger, so you won't be able to call me."

"All right, so I'll talk to you when I talk to you. Tell Willie and Quinn I said hey."

"All right, you straight?"

"Yup, I'm straight. You straight?"

"Yup, I'm straight. All right then, later Slater."

"Later."

Just Checking

Chapter 10

I t's Saturday morning. I decided to call my cousin in Miami to check on Hakeem and Robbie before they started back. "Hello, Quinn, This is your cousin, Gee, from Atlanta. "How you doing?"

"Fine, how you doing?"

"Everything's okay. What you know good?"

"Oh nothing much, just trying to make it."

"Those guys bugging you?"

"No, you know y'all are always welcome. I see you guys so seldom, you know anytime family drops in, it's okay with me."

"Do you mind if I yell at one of them real quick?"

"They're gone already Gee, they left a little less than an hour ago."

"Oh, okay."

"I woke'm up with the smell of breakfast, then they took off. I'm surprised they left so quickly, as late as they stayed up last night."

"Oh, yeah?" A long pause began and followed with a long laboring sigh as if she had something to declare to me.

"Gee, How much does a Ferrari cost?"

"Quinn, You did say 'Ferrari' didn't you?"

"Yes, you know what I'm talking about, the sports car."

"Did your work-a-holic husband go out and buy himself an expensive birthday present? If he did, I guess he owes it to himself as hard as he works. Girl, I didn't know the swimming pool construction business was so good."

"No Gee, a white fellow picked Robbie up in one last night. A new one,… still had the dealers thirty-day tag on it. After Willie and Hakeem went in their direction this guy driving an expensive car like that picked up Robbie and headed in another."

"Who does Robbie know down there like that?"

"That's what I'm trying to figure out myself Gee. You know when people do stuff you don't understand, it makes you wonder bout'm." Our conversation briefly fell silent.

"Quinn, Robbie does a lot of stuff that I don't understand. I'm still trying to figure out why he's still living with your sister as old as his is."

"As close as I can figure, that close call she had with cancer makes him think he has to take care of her."

"But Quinn, that was fifteen years ago and she hasn't had any relapses since."

"Do you think Robbie is doing anything underhanded?" Quinn asked.

"Like what, Cuz."

"Well……" she continued after pausing for a moment. "You know rich, white boys in Miami, with fancy cars makes you wonder. They didn't bother me though. I was in bed after the ten o'clock news, as usual. When Robbie and his buddy came back, they were messing around in the trailer before Hakeem got in, but other than that, they didn't bother me one bit"

"I see. You know this moving company is my baby so I have to check on everybody. You and Willie know what it is to run a business. You got to keep an eye on everything, even relatives."

"Especially relatives," Quinn and I laughed in unison.

"Okay, Quinn, take care and I'll yell atcha when I yell atcha."

"Okay, Gee, y'all be good, bye."

"Okay, bye-bye."

Sunday afternoons are peaceful, casually reading the newspaper and just piddling around the house. I'm thankful I don't have to get up running. Hakeem called just before noon.

"Yo, Homedog, back at the ranch and all is well."

"I hear ya. Everything okay with you?"

"Yup, what you got for me today."

"Man, forget about work today, kick back and take a breather. I know you want to make that Sunday bonus buck, but relax Bro, relax."

"It ain't nut'n but a Gee thang, baby."

"Hey, man, let me yell at you 'bout something."

"Go 'head."

"Last night after you and Uncle Willie made your rounds at the shake-ya-booty-clubs..."

"Yup, you know we did. I got to get the old boy out of the house every now and then. That's about the only joy the old guy gets anymore, Gee. And he be havin a ball, too. I like to see him enjoy himself. He must be a regular at this place he took me. All the ladies know him, and he was spending plenty of money."

"Well, the reason I mention it is because Quinn said that Robbie and some white boy, driving a Ferrari, were messing around in the trailer."

"Oh, yeah?"

"That's what she said. You know Quinn don't miss anything that goes on around there."

"Yeah, she does keep a close reign over the place. You better not come in the house with your shoes on."

"Or go in the kitchen talking 'bout doing the dishes."

"To tell the truth, Gee, I haven't even been in the back of the trailer since we finished loading it and Robbie locked it."

"You did see Robbie lock it?"

"Well...I can't really say, but you and I both know that's his responsibility."

"You know I know, I'm just trying to figure out what reason he would have to go in it."

"You gonna have to talk to him about that, boss."

"Well, if anything is missing or out of place he's the only person that I'm looking at. I tell you what, don't say anything to him about it. I know he's your brother, but he's my cousin, too. If he's up to something, we sure will know about it. When you unload tomorrow morning, be on the lookout for anything fishy."

"I would never think that Slow-motion would be doing anything fishy as far as the customers were concerned."

"I wouldn't either, but I still can't see why he would have any reason to go back in the trailer, unless it was with the customer."

"That's impossible Gee, he left heading towards the ATL when we finished loading, gave me directions, the new address, and said 'bye."

"Okay, Hak, we'll see tomorrow morning when you guys unload. Relax today, Bro, and we'll talk tomorrow.

It's Monday and it's the same routine—work. Sometimes there's serenity in the same routine. Working keeps the mind from being idle. It keeps money in the wallet providing security and a little peace of mind. Lord knows, I can always use a little more. I'm back in the groove of who's got to be where and keeping everybody happy. I get a call from Hakeem. "Yo, Gee, what's up?"

"Another day, another dollar."

"Robbie and I just finished unloading this Miami job and everything is straight. Everything on the inventory list is here. I got certified funds for the balance due and the customer appears to be happy."

"Okay, I'm happy too, then. Tell Robbie I want to talk to him today."

"Now then boss, what else you got for me to do today?"

"Take the rest of the day off and I'll see you tomorrow morning."

"Cool."

"Cool."

Any day that I don't have to physically move furniture I might get some exercise. I might lift weights, go jogging or do a few rounds on my heavy bag. I just finished as the phone rang.

"Yo, Gee, this is Robbie."

"Yo, man, what's up?"

"Hakeem said you wanted to talk to me."

"Yeah, something kinda odd has transacted that I need to ask you about."

"Alright, go ahead."

"When the trailer was parked at Quinn's house, I understand that you and somebody had some reason to go inside. I'm trying to figure out why. I'm trying to figure out how you got in since you're supposed to have locked it, and since Hakeem was supposed to have the key to the door on his key ring. So, enlighten me, please."

"I was showing a buddy of mine how we be making this easy money."

"All right, keep talking."

"What you mean, keep talking?"

"What you mean, what I mean? Come on now Robbie, something is not making sense."

"Gee, what you trip'n 'bout?"

"First of all Robbie, who do you know in Miami other than your Uncle Willie and his family? Secondly, why is the trailer unlocked for you to be 'showing yo buddy how we be making this easy money' at midnight anyway?"

"I met..." Robbie started to reply as I interrupted him.

"Now come on Robbie I got good sense, you know."

"Like I started to say before you interrupted me. I met this guy when we were in Jamaica. You saw him when we were hanging out at The Jungle."

"That blond headed guy trying to dance like he was black?"

"His name is Florida, at least that's what everybody calls him."

"A white boy called Florida?"

"We hit it off pretty good and he told me if I was ever in Florida to look him up. He gave me his business card. The business listed on it is Clifford Williams Chartered Boats."

"Go ahead Robbie, you've got my undivided attention."

"He has a fishing business and you know how I like to fish. He came over Quinn's, picked me up and we hung out for a while. You aughta see his boat! Man... homeboy got it going on, says he be making easy money sometimes, too. He invited me to go fishing with him the next day, no charge, but you know we had to get back here."

"So you and him are best buddies just because you met him in Jamaica?"

"One of those nights your old butt went in early, Florida and I hooked up with some ladies and had a good time. Didn't cost me a dime, homeboy took care of everything. He just likes having somebody to party with. You know how them white boys are; they just like to party. Plenty to smoke, plenty to drink, shoot... money ain't no object to them."

"I'm still trying to figure out why the back of the trailer was unlocked, and whose responsibility is that, I wonder?"

"Since we didn't have our regular truck I didn't even think that Hakeem even had a lock for it, my bad."

"Robbie, you know Hakeem keeps his motorcycles, tools,

and stuff in there ordinarily. How you think he keeps it secure? How are we supposed to keep someone's furniture secure when we have it? Don't be no butterhead now, Robbie."

"My fault boss, nothing got missing. In fact it was a perfect move. Nothing broke, no nothing."

"You lucked up because if anything had gotten missing, guess whose pocket it would have come out of? Not mine."

"Guess who's pocket it would have come out of?" Robbie started mocking me.

"Boy, I'll slap you though this telephone, forget to lock the truck again."

"Hey, man... I'm gonna take Florida up on his boat invitation, you wanna hang?"

"Hang deese nuts, Negro. I got stuff to do and don't be late for work tomorrow morning. Bye Robbie."

"Later, Gee."

The Plan

There are times of the year that people don't move too much, like right after Christmas. The same applies to each month. Some folks are dodging the rent man or some have strategically planned that the end of the month is a good time to move. So usually after the tenth or twelfth, there might be a break that allows time to relax. I have regular customers that call. They might want a room changed around, a piano picked up, anything. We always have things to do. However, the middle of the month can be a time to get away and still not miss out on much money. I decided to jump on my motorcycle for a weekend journey to Ohio. With call forwarding, on these occasions if Hakeem doesn't hang around to answer the phone, I'll ask Freddy to. Getting them to do it is always like pulling teeth though. Freddy being the buckethead that he is will complain that it drives him crazy and Hakeem will insist on answering "hello" like he came straight from the ghetto. I admit that people do call at all times of the day and night, asking stupid questions like "Do you guys cover the furniture when you put it in the truck? Do you have your own truck or do we have to rent one?" I've learned to be patient, take control of the conversation and finish with as little pain as possible. Hakeem and Freddy have not mastered the techniques simply because they're king bucketheads.

After endless weekends and even a thirty-day circle around the U.S., I've gotten one hundred thousand miles on my faithful Goldwing motorcycle. I ride the heck out of the thing and it never complains. Unfortunately I always have to come back to the bump and grind of slinging furniture. I appreciate the breaks. I've arrived back in town, it's Sunday night, and I have to ready the crews for Monday morning.

"Yo, Keem."

"Yo, Gee." We go through our regular Abbot and Costello routine.

"What's up?"

"Nut'n, jus chill'n."

"What's up witchu?"

"Nut'n jus chill'n."

"Yeah?"

"Yeah." A few seconds go by.

"What?"

"What?"

"What you mean what?"

"Oh my bad...What's up?"

"Nut'n, jus chill'n."

"Yeah?

"Yeah, jus chill'n. In the morning?"

"In the morning."

"Later Slater."

"Later Slater."

My calls to the other guys are a little more sane. Big Chuck and Freddy usually just ask what time and say "I'll see you, boss."

"Yo, Robbie, we slinging furniture in the morning, you hanging?"

In a half asleep voice he answered, "Man you should've been with me."

"Sorry for waking you up Bro, I'm trying to get myself together for tomorrow."

"Yeah, I'll be there, but like I said, you should have been with me."

"Yeah, what you been up to? I jumped on my motorcycle and rode up to Ohio. What you been up to?"

"Man you won't believe the fish I caught with my buddy down in Miami."

"I hear you. You been covering some ground too, huh?"

"Gee, my boy Florida knows his stuff about the fishing thing, man."

My group of fellows have been hanging buddies for a while, whether it's motorcycling, pool shooting, or fishing. Robbie's interest was more in fishing then anything else. He likes to watch the fishing shows on television. I never have been one to catch much but my motorcycle camping trips always did include a fishing rod. I could hear how enthusiastic Robbie was in his voice.

"I brought back two coolers slam full of red snapper, sea bass and a couple of somethings that I don't even know the names of. Gee I'm telling you man, this guy knows the ropes, and his boat is off the chain, forty-four foot, Gulf Craft Sport Fisherman...

"All right, all right, Bro, I feel you. Homeboy got you all excited and stuff. Sounds like you bout creamed yo pants."

"I'm talking about for real, Gee, more than once and I ain't even ashamed."

"Well I'm glad you enjoyed yourself. You hook me up with a big ass red snapper and one or two of them somethings that you don't know the name of and that'll be all right wit me."

"No problem, Mon," Robbie imitated a Jamaican accent, "ain't no way I can eat all this fish I caught. I'll be going back down there before long anyway."

"Bring me some tomorrow when you come to work."

"All right that'll work."

Hakeem called back. It had been a couple of days since I had seen him.

"Yo, Gee, you home man? I got some money I need to get out of my hands."

Gerald Randolph Howard

"Yeah, man, I'm here. You stopping by?"

"Yeah, I'll be there in about twenty minutes."

I can always hear Hakeem before he gets to the house because he plays his music so loud. I opened the garage door, which leads to the lower portion where my office is.

"Yo, Homeboy, why you gotta play that rap junk so loud?" I turned my hat sideways and grabbed my crotch imitating his music's lifestyle. "You be messing up my Rick and Teena before you even get in the neighborhood."

We took care of business and as usual had to challenge each other at a game of pool. "Come on in here and take this tail whooping Bro, it ain't nothing new," Hakeem started the challenge. "And why don't you put on some real music?"

I grabbed my pool stick as a microphone and sang along, "I'm just a sucka for your love." Walking around the table I sympathized, " Young folk don't even know what real music is. And you know darn well you can't beat a man on his own table. I don't know why you keep trying. I'm just a sucka for your love."

"If my memory is correct I did it the last time we played and the time before that and the time before that." "See I told you about smoking that heathen devil weed marajawana. You can't remember doo-doo. You and your brother are two of the dope smokin'est rascals I ever met."

"Don't put me in the same category with him. I might take a hit every now and then but that boy got it bad.

I got to the chorus of the song now.

>"Oh you're a real sexy little thing
>
>And you make my whole heart sing,
>
>And there's not in this world that I wouldn't do...
>
>I'm just a sucka for your love"

I took the first shot but nothing fell in.

"Yeah, looks like the same old story; Gee takes a whooping on his own table again."

"It's your shot, Bro, and don't be scratching the felt." I insisted.

"You got some of that fish Robbie brought back from Miami?" Hakeem inquired.

"Not yet, but he talks like he's got quite a bit."

"You know that's the same guy he was hanging with down in Jamaica." Hakeem continued.

"Yeah and the same guy Robbie had messing around in the back of your trailer. The guy runs a fishing business down in Miami. By Robbie's account, he's got it going on." I explained.

"Robbie swears by the guy, supposed to be going with him the next time he goes to Jamaica."

"What...?"

"He said he'd take anyone that wants to go for a hundred bucks. Five ball in the side pocket."

Hakeem hit the shot but the eight ball fell in also, losing by default. "Damn... whooped that booty again. Like I said how you gonna beat a man on his own table? Grab the rack, Sucka, you know the routine."

"You know you about a lucky ..."

"Like I said, grab the rack," I remarked throwing salt on Keem's wound.

"I wouldn't mind making that trip, Gee, if we could swing it."

"What you mean, 'if we could swing it'?"

"Well, you know something like that would take at least eight days or so. And besides, you know you my running buddy. How am I gonna do something like that without you?"

"Oh, you gonna automatically include me in a boat ride to Jamaica cause I'm yo running buddy?"

"Well, you know we be going on our trips together. We'd have to take the time off work and you know you got yo girl over there."

"Well, what do you know about Robbie's boy that owns the boat?"

"To tell you the truth, Gee, I've never really talked to him except for a second on the dance floor at the Jungle. I'm just going by what Robbie has come up with. From what I can tell about all those fish he came back with, he must know his boating business. I doubt that homeboy would own a forty-foot boat and not know what he's doing."

"Hey, Keem, what you think a boat like that cost?"

"I don't know, but homeboy got to be banked like Hank, driving a Ferrari."

"Yo, man, what I got high or low balls?"

"Your last girlfriend said you got low balls." Hakeem replied amusing himself. "What's the matter, you can't talk and play at the same time? You got the high ones. It's my shot anyway."

"When is this trip supposed to be happening?"

"I really don't know, Robbie's the one with the contact. It's his buddy, you know. Shoot, if we can get the whole wrecking crew together it would be quite an adventure."

"You know how boats and me don't go together Hakeem."

"They got stuff you can take Gee." He replied mocking me.

"I know. I'm okay just as long as they keep moving. It's when they stop and all that darn rocking and rolling starts happening is what gets me. The last time I was on a boat was with The Black Angels when we rode to Key West. It was my fault, though, I ate like a pig just before we went out. Man I couldn't figure out which end of my body wanted to dispel its contents first."

"You mean you didn't know if you wanted to puke or dook."

"I barfed so bad I thought I was going to pass out. I'm talking about for real man, thought I was going to pass out!"

"From what I understand, it takes like fifteen hours to get around Cuba to Montego Bay.

"As long as we keep moving the kid will be all right." I repeated in an attempt to convince myself.

"We can kick the idea around, maybe yell at Freddy, see if he might be game for it."

"Speaking of kick'n and game, yours sucks right about now soul Brotha number-one. Eight ball in the corner." I made sure to take good aim on this shot. This was one of the rare occasions I won two games straight. The shot fell perfectly in the hole. "Bam! Boy, I am not playing you any more. This is getting boring. You just can't play. I don't know who said that you could shoot pool. I'm just not gonna play you anymore Keem."

"Yeah, yeah, yeah. Man, please, I gave you one game and you lucked up and won one. I'll grab the rack; I'm good for another game."

"Look, man, what part did you not understand? I told you I am not playing you anymore. You are no competition. You suck... You stink... and your momma don't wear no mink. Ah ha, ah ha." I held my stomach and faked a laugh. "I got other things to do. Let me go see if my refrigerator is still running. I got to get a haircut. Oh, I forgot I don't have any hair. I know you hate it... you got yo booty whooped again!"

"Oh, okay, Buckethead, I'm gonna let you have your day today. You lucked up today. Next time we gonna play for money. Then we gonna see who 'The Man' is."

"Yeah, but till then you gotta take your no pool shooting booty up outta here." Hakeem headed out through the garage. "And close the door behind you."

I had picked up a calling card earlier in the day anticipating talking to Jacy later in the evening.

"Hello," Jacy's niece answered the phone.

"Hey, bebop, this is Gee, how are you today?"

"Fine, tank you."

Mika's young voice reminds me that I'm talking to a little person. "Did you go to school today?"

"Yes."

"Is everything okay?"

"Yes, tank you."

"Is Jacy there?"

"Yes, one moment please."

"Hello," Jacy answered."

"Hey, Baby, how are you?"

"The love of my life. Me doing okay, guess what."

"Okay, let me think... you won the lottery?"

"No, you know me no have de money to trow away on stuff like dat."

"Oh, darn, I was hoping we were rich all of a sudden and I could stop lifting this heavy tail furniture. You know I'm getting older by the minute."

"If me knew de right potion to mix, dat would be me next concoction. Besides you know me can't play de game where me sell de tickets."

"Okay, let me guess again. You been missing me and you can't wait another minute to see me."

"Exactly right. Wow... me telepathy is rubbing off on you! You took de words right out of me mout mon."

"Something told me that would be a safe guess. As a matter of fact, Jacy, I been missing you too girl. What have you been up too?"

"Well, Gee, you know me routine, me do de same ting almost everyday. Me try to stay positive and be tankful of de blessings me have, a job and a roof over me head. Me dreams are of being wit you someday. Rubbing yo bald head and cooking yo favorite dish for you."

"I like the head rubbing part, tell me more."

"Me see rubbing yo head and telling you dat everyting is going to be all right. In fact Me tink dat is going to happen before long. If it were up to me, yo head would be on me lap right now. Me do have a feeling that me going to see you before long, Gee. Me dream you were coming to see me on a boat."

"Huh?"

"Yup. Me vivid dreams lately have been of you and a white mon on a boat. T'ree nights straight now and de weight of yo bald head on me stomach has disturbed me in de middle of de night. De setting of a peaceful boat trip in de moonlight wit dis mon at de helm would be an interesting adventure for you and yo friends. But me feel uncomfortable about de weight of someting."

"Jacy, have you been talking to one of my gang lately?" I ask knowing her well enough to know she doesn't have access to any of their phone numbers.

"No, what you mean, Mon?"

"You are tripping me out girl, because Robbie has a white friend that has a boat. He has given us an invitation to go with him on his next trip there."

"Yeah?"

"I'm just trying to figure which one of these guys you have been talking to, Jacy."

"No, Mon, me no talk to any of dem. Me tell you if me did. Gee, you are de love of me life, I keep no secrets from you. You know dat."

"I'm flabbergasted that you have had dreams like that. It's like you've been reading my mind Sweetheart."

"See, our spirits are closer den you tink, Mr. Howell. You tink me lie when me say dat me tink of you de first ting in de morning and de last ting at night?"

"I can't believe you have been having dreams like this, Jacy. Tell me more."

"Dere is noting more to tell Gee, but me tink dat you should come. Me long to see you so bad."

"I hadn't given it much thought. It's just something Robbie has stumbled upon. Hakeem and I were talking about the invitation earlier today. You still got me tripping, though."

"Living here on dis island we see all kinds of boats, dey come and go. Tis noting new to us, Mon. If dey can do it, you can too. Would you please come, Gee? Please... please... please... Me miss you so much?"

"How did we get started talking about this anyway, girl?"

"Me just telling you about me dreams, Gee, please come."

"Yeah, well I'm still flipped out that you would be having dreams like this... wow."

Our conversation proceeded with the normal chitchat that sweethearts talk about for a few more minutes until a business call came. I try not to miss calls because they're most generally about money. I have an obligation to more people than myself to keep busy. If I'm not scheduling appointments, the boys aren't making anything. If someone had been able to see me, they would have asked why my mouth fell open when Jacy told me about her dream. It struck me as an amazing coincidence that she had such a dream. I'm not one to believe in psychics, voodoo this or voodoo that. I don't believe the junk people say about Jamaican's burying your underwear. I'm not about to drink any root juice to "make my nature stand up like a donkey." I guess I'm real skeptical. Other than faith in the Lord, if I can't see it, touch it, hear it, I don't put much faith in it. To say the least, Jacy's dream had tripped me out.

OK, Let's Do It

Chapter 12

During the real busy times of the month I need every available body, including mine. Today will be the last day of a ten-day grind and I've done the last four days with them. Being the boss, I get to pick and choose who works with whom. Taking into consideration that I am the oldest, I try to take guys with me that can take the workload off me. I prefer to take it easy. I had Freddy and Moreno with me on this particular day. Freddy has a lot of experience and I'm about the only one that can communicate adequately with Moreno, because he doesn't speak much English. Having been married previously to a Puerto Ricania inspired me to practice my high school Spanish lessons. Of course the more you practice anything, the better you get. I always liked the advantage to be able to speak and not have anyone else know what we were talking about. Moreno was an excellent employee and doubled as my occasional Spanish teacher. I can't deny that our Mexican American brothers have an excellent work ethic and Moreno works his butt off. I'm not particularly concerned about his immigration status. I appreciate him because I can trust him and he doesn't complain. As we pulled out of the parking lot Freddy shouted. "Yo, Gee!"

"Freddy, why do you have to talk so loud? I'm sitting right here."

"My bad."

"Can you say buckethead?"

Moreno understood how we used the word 'buckethead' and chuckled.

Freddy confessed. "I'm a buckethead."

"Now try it again and not so loud please."

"Why you didn't say anything to me about you guys going to Jamaica on Florida's boat? I thought we were running buddies?"

"I haven't committed to anyone about going anywhere on anybody's boat. I understand that Robbie's buddy said it would be all right with him if we wanted to ride, for a hundred bucks. Other then talking to Hakeem about it, I haven't said anything more about it." I decided to keep it to myself about Jacy's dream.

"Oh, I thought you were going to have me answering the phone and running things while the wrecking crew went off exploring the world."

"Like I said, I hadn't thought too much more about it."

"Well I kind of investigated it a little, and it seems like it would be an easy trip, weather permitting. Going around the eastern side of Cuba, between Haiti south through the Windward Passage would put you on the east side of Jamaica. A couple of hours more would put you on the west side near Mo Bay."

"Well get-on-down, Brotha. I guess you have been studying it, talking about countries and passages and junk. Oh, you're a first class navigator now?" Even though Freddy displayed frequent and obvious signs of the medical term 'buckethead-itis,' he had always been a rather technical person.

"If he didn't have enough fuel to make the whole trip, there are plenty of places in Cuba to gas up."

"Okay."

"Okay? What you mean, okay?" I figured you of all people would be game for something like that. Mr. Ride a Motorcycle all the way around the United States, Mr. Parachute out of an Airplane, Mr. Karate..."

"Freddy."

"What?"

"Close yo face. We got some furniture to move today and that's what is on my mind right now."

Moreno in his broken English said, "Yeah, Buckethead."

We all cracked up. Suddenly, Freddy ran a red light and slammed on the brakes, barely missing two people crossing the street.

I hurriedly rolled down the window and leaned my head out. "Sorry, fellows, our fault," I called out. One guy gave us the finger and the other held his arms outstretched, pantomiming "Damn, didn't you see us?" I think I was more shaken then they were.

> "All right fellows," I said, pulling my head back in. "Let's get serious. We can act stupid later." Visibly shaken, it took us a few minutes to regain our composure.

After thirty seconds of complete silence, Moreno said, "Buckethead."

At seven o'clock in the evening, I wasn't really interested in talking to customers or employees. The phone rang my private number; it was Hakeem.

> "Yo, Gee."

> "Yo, Keem, what's up?"

> "Hey, man, turn that old folks' music down in the background so you can hear."

> "Huh? Wait a minute, I gotta turn the music down in the background so I can hear." I put the phone down and came back ten seconds later. "Yo, Homeskillet, what it is?" I asked in my black pimp dialect.

> "Me, Robbie, and Freddy are hanging out at the Mexican restaurant watching the Falcons game. You want me to pick you up?"

> "No, man, I got something sexy coming over in a little while."

> "Oh, so you can't hang wit da boys tonight, huh?"

> "Like I said, I got some company coming over and to tell you the truth, she looks a whole lot better than all three of y'all put together. She got big, pretty, luscious breast-est-ses."

"Hey, man, what's the schedule look like the next week or so?"

"Oh! And she got a big booty too."

"I know we just got past the beginning of the month rush."

"Yeah, we been hanging and that's the truth. Why you ask me that? Wait, let me answer that question. I got ESP and I'll bet you guys are going to accept Florida's invitation to go to Jamaica on his boat?"

"Thinking seriously about it."

"Something told me that was on your mind." I concluded.

"If we got the time, I'm game if you are. Professor Freddy seems to have it all figured out."

"Freddy doesn't know the first thing about navigating a boat from one side of the tub to the other."

"Well, between him and Robbie's faith in Florida, it sounds possible." Hakeem reasoned.

"People do it all the time, Keem, I know it's possible. To tell the truth, I only have enough for one truck for the next few days. If Big Chuck doesn't mind taking a few days off after those jobs are done, then it sounds like a plan, weather permitting."

"We've been watching the weather south of Florida throughout the Caribbean, and it looks okay."

"Although it could change in a week's time Keem."

"Yeah, I guess it could. If it does, we'll just have to play with all those fine, sexy, Jamaican girls a little longer then planned."

"Hey, man, when is Florida planning on going?"

"The day after tomorrow."

"You got your hundred bucks?"

"Yup."

"Well, I got mine." The doorbell rang. "Alright,Homeskillet,

I gotta run. My lady friend is here."

"Hey, Gee, you aren't gonna back out now, are you?"

"You know, Jacy has been bugging me to show my face, so this might be a good opportunity." I answered the door with phone in hand. "Come in. Hey, man, I'll talk to you later. I got something to do. Bye"

Before I go out of town, there are a few things I have to do to just to have peace of mind. Cut the grass, suspend newspaper service, ask my neighbor to clear out my mailbox every few days. I changed my answering service to say that I'd be out of town and to please call back on a certain date. Since this was Robbie's acquaintance, his connection, he was the host. We all met at his house and piled into a cargo van he had borrowed. We anticipated bringing back some fish. Between fours guys, a suitcase a piece and coolers to haul back our catch, we needed the extra room. For the next ten hours, we took turns sleeping, driving, telling lies, and anticipating what we were going to be getting into. None of us had ever spent more than a fishing trip's time on a boat, much less crossed some water. We all thought of it as an adventure. Over the years the guys have come to be a little more adventurous simply by listening to my accounts of mine. I'd always challenge Hakeem to ride his motorcycle with me further than his usual barhopping. That was the difference between his type of bike and mine. Those crotch rockets have you aching from bending over in such a crouched position. Freddy has always talked about parachuting. I've listened for years to him talking about what he was going to do. My reply has always been, "What you waiting for? Just do it." I almost don't understand Robbie's motivation. I know he likes to fish. As a matter fact, I don't think his television plays anything other than fishing programs. But other than that, I'm surprised he'd venture out on something like this. Shoot, the guy, still lives with his Momma, which tells a lot.

Gerald Randolph Howard

The Trip

Chapter 13

Robbie told us Florida planned to leave sometime after sunset. I understood that the ocean would be calmer at that time. It was the middle of September, and I guess the position of the moon and time of year all had something to do with the tides. I was putting my trust in other folks on this one; namely Florida, by way of Robbie. He did own a boating business and I did see him in Jamaica on a previous trip. I was definitely not in control at all. I know that you have to have faith in the mailman to do his job and bring the mail. When you go to the doctor, you have to have faith that he knows what he's cutting on. So, to me, it takes faith in other people just to make it in the world; no doubt about it. As we drew near our destination, Robbie made a call to let Florida know that we were close.

The marina had some fine boats, to say the least. I always wonder what kind of people can afford such luxurious items. Everybody wasn't in the fishing business to have their boats pay for themselves. Some folks just have money. I can't be mad at them. There were about a hundred of them, some bigger than others, some with sails, some old, some just absolutely gorgeous. We pulled into a parking space at the marina, got out, and followed Robbie to Florida's boat. I had once gone on a day fishing trip with my motorcycle buddies, but this boat was even bigger than that one. I was instantly impressed. Two men were on the deck talking, one of whom looked familiar. I remembered him to be the guy dancing and hanging out with Robbie. We caught his attention as we approached.

"Yo, fellas, I'm glad you made it. Robbie, how you doing?"
They grasped hands and hugged as if they were good

friends. It caught my attention that the Isley Brothers were playing on the boat's stereo system.

"Fine, man, good to see you again."

"You ready to party in the sunshine again?"

"Man, I can't wait, I think you remember my gang that was with me at the jungle. This is my brother Hakeem, my boss Gee, and buddy Freddy." Everybody shook hands with our guide and exchanged greetings.

"Okay, since everybody is here, you and the guys can get your stuff and load up; we're ready to roll, Brotha."

I thought this guy was trying to sound black, calling Robbie "Brotha."

"Sounds good to me," Robbie replied.

"Keep in mind that we don't want to take any unnecessary stuff, just the bare necessities."

"Yeah, I already explained that to the guys. I think we got it down pat."

"Make sure your car is secure. Here, stick this on your dash to let the marina know that you are one of my guests. You can bring some music if you want, I got a kick'n stereo system. I know you got some good R&B. Florida handed Robbie a piece of paper with some bold lettering on it.

"Sure, man, I got plenty of music."

Besides the four Musketeers making the trip, there was another group of five people - two women and three men - already on board. One gentleman I observed talking to Florida seemed to be the leader of the bunch, maybe forty years old. The others looked old enough to be his parents. The five spoke Spanish among themselves. I wondered if any of them spoke English. They seemed cordial, responding with polite smiles every time we made eye contact. I guessed they were Cuban.

It didn't take long for us to grab our one bag each. Robbie began untying ropes and assisting our new friend in backing the big rig away from the dock. I think out of respect for our traveling partners, Florida put on some easy listening music, and we were off. He guided the boat through the lanes toward the open water with Robbie beside him as if he were a co-captain. Their silhouettes looked majestic in the moonlight, making the scene picturesque. Robbie held the steering wheel for a minute while Florida walked out to make an announcement. He spoke in English and Spanish, "My home is your home. Mi casa es su casa, ladies and gentleman. Our first stop is Cabo Lucrecia Cuba. Nosotros primera parada es Capo Lucrecia Cuba. We ought to get there around daylight. Debier de llegar de la manana. So find a comfortable spot. Entonces encontra unsitio comodo. The bathroom is downstairs on the right, before you get to the bedroom. El bano esta baho a dereche antes el cuarto de cama. Anything you need, just ask and I'll try to accommodate you the best I can. Qual quiera pregunta me y trato da le el mejor que puedo." He quickly returned to the controls.

I guessed Florida to be between thirty-five and forty years old, about five-foot ten, a hundred and eighty pounds. He appeared to be either street wise, or had hung around black people when he was growing up. His announcement answered the question of whether or not our traveling companions spoke English. He took aggressive authority in an efficient, capable manner. This was quite a different character than the one I had perceived grooving on the dance floor.

Hakeem and I sat side by side on a bench seat in the open air. A few minutes after departing, Hakeem whispered, "Yo Gee, I see El Capitan be making a buck or two when he's not fishing. I wonder what my man is charging these folks?"

"Yeah, Keem, I see. It doesn't take much to see that Homeboy is about making money. I can't be mad at him. You know we make money with trucks. He does it with his boat. You know, I was wondering how he could afford to drive this big thing all the way down to Jamaica on just four hundred dollars. Freddy says it holds about two hundred gallons of gas. That's five hundred just to fill the bad boy up. Ain't no telling how much it actually takes to get there."

"You know what, Gee, I'll bet Florida is charging them a

whole lot more than one hundred bucks a piece."

"Yeah, how you figure, Keem?"

"Because if we're stopping in Capo whatever, with some folks that don't appear to be going to party in Jamaica, I'll bet Homeboy is carrying these folks back to Cuba on the downlow."

"Smuggling, and there's no telling what's in all those boxes."

"Call it what you wanna. You know the U.S. has economic sanctions against Cuba."

"How you know about economic sanctions Keem, I didn't teach you that?"

"Oh I can teach you a thing or two also, Gee Buckethead."

"Hey, why I gotta be a buckethead? It made sense to me leaving at night cause the ocean is calmer. But maybe there was another reason that we didn't know about."

"Ain't no telling. I don't know Homeboy well enough to ask him."

"Me, either. As long as he gets us to Jamaica with no problems, I'm straight."

"Me too, Gee, I can't be mad at him for making his money. You know when we get a chance to run out of state on the downlow, we'll do it, too, if the money is right and we don't foresee any problems."

"As long as we been slinging furniture, we know the ropes well enough to bend the rules every now and then. Like I said, I'm straight as long as we don't have any problems."

"Man, I'm glad I got this jacket on, it's get'n a little chilly."

"I tell you what, I stayed up super late last night just so I would be dead tired and go to sleep on this sucker. Besides the more I'm unaware of what's swaying back and forth, the better I'll be. I do not feel like barfing tonight."

"You gonna jump in one of those beds." Hakeem

inquired.

"Yup, Florida did say make ourselves at home, didn't he?"

"Well, don't be surprised if I double up one with you. There's not a whole lot of sleeping room available for everyone, and don't be touching my booty, either."

"Well, I'm entitled to touch the booty that is usually beside me in bed. So I can't guarantee what I might do half-asleep."

"A ha a ha," Hakeem faked a laugh. "Like I said, don't be touching my booty, Sugar."

The further we got away from land, the darker it got. A full moon provided the only outside light available. The boat had adequate lights in front and throughout the interior. Until daylight there wasn't going to be any sightseeing, just blackness. It seemed as though we would have a smooth ride. There weren't any huge waves to climb, nothing tossing us around too much. I figured that the steady forward motion kept us level. The music mixed with the constant sounds of the engines and the sea. Relating this to my motorcycling lifestyle, I understood how someone could get into boating, especially if you could make money at it. It definitely wasn't your average nine-to-five occupation. Crossing a body of water would be a first time experience for me. This was all new, another notch in my belt. At least when it was over, I'd be able to say that I had ridden a boat other than an ocean liner across a sizable amount of water. Surely the Pacific ocean was not next on my list. I found my way to one of the bedrooms and curled into a fetal position that allowed me to put myself out of any potential misery. That's exactly what my last boating experience had been, miserable.

I was jarred awake by a commotion upstairs on the deck. It took me a second to realize that I wasn't at home in my bed. The boat had stopped. Gathering my consciousness and equilibrium, I headed up to see what was happening. To my surprise, Florida and a couple of the men on board were trying to subdue a huge fish that was flopping around on the deck. The battle amazed me. After a couple of heavily wielded strokes with a metal bar, it was over.

"Now, that's a fish!" Freddy yelled.

Florida answered, "It's an amberjack. Open the hatch, Robbie."

Robbie opened the door that let the big fish fall into a holding area.

I could see that they had some trolling lines stretched out in the water. There was one on each side of the boat. Obviously they had been fishing for a good little while.

"Yo, Gee, you been missing the fun, man," Robbie called out excitedly.

"I see."

"Check this out," he exclaimed as I peered inside the well.

"Whoa! Y'all been throwing down." There were approximately thirty fish of different varieties and sizes. The last one was the biggest."

"Yeah, it takes a little more effort to land one of those." Florida explained. "This is a nice sized one. It might be thirty pounds." Without hesitation, he headed back to the wheel and started moving us forward again.

I assumed all the Spanish folks were in the other room sleeping. None were on the deck. It was still dark and the moon was still high in the sky. "Yo, man, how long I been asleep?"

Robbie replied, "I don't know, a few hours I'm sure."

"Darn, I was hoping you'd say we were almost there."

"Boy, you sound like a little kid going on vacation with momma and daddy. 'Are we there yet Daddy?' Sit back, relax, and enjoy the ride."

"Man, how am I going to enjoy the ride when I'm wondering if I'm going to be sick any minute? It's pitch black out here and I can't see a thing."

"Man... riding, listening to good music, I'm having a ball.

Hey, come upstairs to the bow and check out what's happening."

I followed Robbie.

"Yo, man, you get enough sleep?" Florida asked me.

"I tried to stay up late last night so I would be sleepy. If I had woken up just as you were pulling into Capo whatever it is you said, I'd be straight."

Florida chuckled and said, "it's Capo Lucrecia."

"Yo, Gee, didn't you have a girlfriend named Lucrecia back in the 'hood?" Robbie cracked.

"Yup, you remember her. She tattooed my name on her back. You used to go with her sister Zakina."

"Yeah, right."

"Yo, Brotha, how about taking over the wheel for a minute?" Florida offered.

"No, man, I'll leave that up to you professionals."

"Aw, man, it's easier than you think. Here," he said, stepping to the side and handing me the wheel. "All you have to do is keep these navigational marks between here and here." He pointed with his index finger. "Yo Robbie, it looks like we got another fish on the right-side line. You wanna check it out?" Florida asked as he slowed the boat a little.

"Got him boss, if I need help, I'll yell," Robbie said over his shoulder as he headed to the lower level.

Our captain spoke first to initiate a conversation. "Robbie was telling me you get seasick sometimes."

"Yup, barfed up a storm the last time. I was taking flying lessons years ago and it hit me up there, too. Needless to say, I didn't get my license."

"Funny how motion sickness hits some people and

other people are not affected at all." He commented, going through his compact disc holder. "How 'bout some Prince?"

I shook my head affirmatively. "I like your taste in music. I wish I was one of the 'other people,' 'cause the last time, I thought I was gonna die."

"I got some stuff in my first aid kit if it starts to hit you."

"Oh, don't worry, I got this patch behind my ear and enough Dramamine to start a store. I didn't put anything on my stomach before we started out, either. Unfortunately I'm getting hungry right about now."

"We'll be pulling into Capo's docks in a few hours or so. I got some folks there that will give us something to eat. As a matter of fact, that's where the fish and these other folks are going. It'll be about a two-hour stop and we'll keep on pushing. It will give you a chance to take a break, walk around a little. Just don't wander off too far."

"How often do you make it down this way?" I asked curiously.

"Every now and then. It's kinda my regular stop when I'm in the Caribbean. I feel comfortable stopping at the same places."

Robbie came back to the helm and pushed the throttle forward to resume the previous speed. "Another sea bass. Those are some nice fish, Gee."

"Isn't that what you gave me the last time you went fishing?"

"No, the last time we were fishing on the bottom. We got a lot of snapper then," Florida explained.

"All right, Bro, I'll let you take over now." I meant for Florida to take over, but Robbie stepped right up to the wheel.

"See, it's not so hard," Florida remarked.

"Whoa! That was a big one!" I said, as the sea tossed the boat around."

"No it wasn't, man, that was just another little wave." Florida said.

"It was little to you, but it was big to me. If you don't mind me asking, what's a rig like this set you back?"

"Not as much as you might think. I got it at a bankruptcy sale. With the repairs I had to do to it, I only have about fifty thou in it. It's ten years old."

"Man, this bad boy looks brand new." Obviously Florida was a stickler for neatness by the way he kept the boat.

"Thanks, this is my baby. I try to take care of her the best I can. Besides, this is my moneymaker. I take better care of her than my car. That thing don't make a dime."

"I hear ya, Bro. I'm the same way about my trucks. And they don't go anywhere unless they're making money."

"I'm the same way, Gee."

I could feel the beauty of operating this big powerful vehicle. For some reason, we men are passionate about our authority over machines; the bigger the better, it seems. I'm just as much at fault as anyone with the fancy cars and motorcycles I have owned. I had once envisioned owning a small plane, but the motion sickness thing took care of that. Our conversation helped to pass the time.

Before long, I saw the sun starting to rise on the southeast corner of the horizon. There couldn't have been a more picturesque sight than its steady advance. Occasionally, a wave would bury it back into the horizon. After a few more minutes, even the biggest waves couldn't reach that high. Land was within sight. The first part of our adventure was coming to an end. It had proven to be not so bad after all. I concluded this was all right. I might like this after all. Florida made a forty-five degree turn toward the shore, and within minutes, we were pulling up to a wooden dock that looked to be someone's private property. It extended about one hundred feet into the water. We were in a remote area with the feel of a small town or village.

The shore was dotted with fishing boats, most of them small, able to hold maybe four people, anchored half on the shore and half in the water. By now, everyone on the boat was awake. The other group was talking among themselves and excitedly pointing to the shore. As we approached a small group of people began appearing to greet the boat. One of the grandmotherly ladies onboard shrieked with joy, and was answered by one of the ladies on shore.

Freddy eased all forty-four feet precisely parallel to the dock. Robbie, performing his first-mate duties, secured a big rope to the rear of the boat. The three Cuban men helped the ladies off to hugs and greetings from the people on shore. They were all extremely happy to see each other. I guessed they hadn't seen each other in years. Tears flowed, which gave me the impression that my guess was correct. One of the female passengers was so overwhelmed with joy that she collapsed into the welcoming arms. They laid her down on the wooden surface and everyone hovered over her. Hats came off and were used to fan her. Someone yelled "da le agua por favor." I grabbed some bottled water and a hand towel from the john and delivered them quickly. She was coherent enough to take a few sips. The men helped her sit up, then stand. She managed to walk with supporting arms encircling her, toward the early morning solitude of the village. She didn't appear to be ready for any more celebrating.

My gang got off to stretch. This was our chance to get off the boat for a little while. Florida spoke, "Yo, fellas, there's a little fish store/hangout with a bathroom right there." He pointed to a haggard-looking little building across the road. "In fact, they'll fry us up some of these fish we caught if you want. I'll meet you over there in about fifteen minutes. Oh, and it'll help if someone could speak Spanish."

I answered him saying that I had it, "Yo lo tango."

> "Bien," he yelled back, as he headed towards a makeshift office building at the head of the dock.

Capo Lucretia

Chapter 14

O bviously, Florida was well-known here. Four men came to help unload the boat. Our gang formed an assembly line with two guys getting the boxes. Two older men slowly started unloading the fish into a makeshift cart that looked like it was on it's last leg. The two old guys looked like they were too. "If someone don't help the Burrito Brothers, we gonna be here all day," Freddy cracked.

Hakeem replied. "Freddy."

"What?"

"You a Buckethead. You can help them if you want, but I'm sure they know what they doing."

"Oh I believe they know what they doing, it just looks like they gonna take all day doing it."

I interrupted, "Let'm take a while, fellas, I could use a break anyway."

Robbie got in the conversation, "I'm proud of you, Gee, you held it down like a real soldier."

"Yeah, and even though I'm starvin like Marvin, I am not gonna overdo it either so I can keep holding it down."

Stretching our muscles and legs to revive ourselves, we headed across the road. This looked like a Mom and Pop, family type store. It had the feel of a general store. Cluttered shelves displayed food for purchase. Most of it looked freshly picked: bananas, onions, rutabagas, and stuff I didn't even know the names of. From this vantage point, it may have been the only store in the village. The kitchen was an open display also. It was well used, to say the least.

The hanging pots and pans looked like something someone's grandma used. The air smelled like fresh coffee mixed with the tobacco leaves hanging on the wall. There were plenty of flies. Florida arrived at the same time as the old men with the fish.

He greeted Mom and Pop, as if they were old friends. Mom, a short, little, gray haired lady, reached up to hold Florida's cheeks, and kissed each one. In Spanish, he asked her to fry some of the fish for our group. She smiled and instructed the two slow moving old men which fish to take out back to clean. Before long, she had the place smelling like Cabaña's Restaurant on Ponce, back in Atlanta. As early as half past daybreak, Mom and Pop had the place alive. Genuine salsa music filled the air from a worn radio hanging from the ceiling. "How you like my spot fellas?" Florida asked.

"Mom and Pop got it going on, Bro," Hakeem replied. "That fish gonna be swing'n. What we gonna have with it?"

"Don't worry, Mom gonna hook us up. She does it every time I'm here. She'll probably have some mixed vegetables, Cuban bread. I guarantee you'll like it. These are some of the sweetest people in the world."

Florida was right; Mom gave us a treat, Cuban style. Even though fish wasn't exactly breakfast food for me, it was delicious. There was plenty of it too, unfortunately, I had to keep in mind that me, a full stomach, and a boat wasn't exactly a good mix. I ate just enough to kill the hungries, and I was straight. The boys proceeded to stuff their faces.

I cautioned, "All right, don't y'all be wasting that good food in the ocean. Cause as bad as you guys ribbed me about getting seasick, I'm gonna laugh my booty off if I hear the first sound of upchuck'n."

Nobody said a word; they just kept feeding their faces. "And if you do get sick don't be asking me for any of my drugs to make you feel better," I added.

Hakeem and Freddy raised up with mouths full, looked at each other, and went back to eating.

Robbie asked Florida, " Hey, man, you want that last piece of fish?"

"Naw, go 'head, man."

I stood up and laid a ten spot on the table.

Florida said, "Yo, Gee, you don't have to do that here. It's already taken care of."

"Oh, yeah?"

"See, I barter with the fish we caught. If I give them the fish, we get fed. We may have had about two hundred pounds of fish with us. It buys a little bit of fuel also."

"Well, I want to show Mom that I appreciate her good cooking. I don't mind. Guess I'll head back towards the boat."

"Gee, why don't you head back towards the boat?" Freddy cracked.

With mouths full, they all started laughing as I walked away.

Mumbling, out loud, I imitated a neurotic crackhead as I quickly stepped. I made sure they could hear me, "I hope y'all clowns get so sick that it starts coming outcha moufs and booty holes at the same time...till you can't barf no more... I hope y'all barf at the same time... in harmony... yeah, I'm gonna laugh my booty off... dat's right... I'mo laugh." I could still hear them snickering as I walked out of earshot.

Florida's Blues

Chapter 15

leisurely hung around the boat, enjoying the scenery. This gave me the opportunity to let my food settle so I wouldn't have any problems later. I was looking forward to seeing Jacy. Out of all my visits, this one was going to trip her out the most. I had only briefly mentioned that we were considering coming on a boat. I didn't really know until the last minute that we might actually do this. Jacy welcomes my visits so much that she allows me to drop in anytime. I get a kick out of the expression on her face when I catch her unexpectedly. She gets embarrassed that she's not prepared. I might catch her with either no makeup, or in some house clothes that aren't so flattering. After the hugs and kisses, she settles down. I know it's an unwritten rule to call before I come, but I guess this is my way of implementing exclusive privilege. We men ought to be ashamed of ourselves with the double standards we employ sometimes. Some of us would throw fits if our lady friends would just pop in unannounced. I think we use it to address our insecurity about not knowing if we're the only ones they are keeping company with.

Jacy has proven to me that she is crazy about me. Through her letters and open door policy, I've always felt at home in her home. Besides, I stayed there openly, in the presence of her father and niece. The family knew we were together. I doubt very much if she would allow another man to be privileged to such circumstances in front of her family. I never doubted her devotion or morals. Jacy has always displayed the traits of a fine, upstanding woman. I love her accent, and the pampering and attention she gives me. For the longest, I've suggested that one day she'd be allowed to visit me and I would reciprocate. It would be a joy to see her in my territory, and watch the expression on her face when she sees how other people live. I imagine it would be a culture shock. We lived worlds apart and I would like to at least share the experience of mine with her. The things that some people take for granted, others might appreciate. I would get a big kick out of showing Jacy how I lived. Besides, she was a good person and deserved to be pampered and indulged.

In ten minutes, the wrecking crew was standing on the dock. Florida showed up shortly afterward, with a worried look on his face. "Yo, Bro, everything okay?" Robbie asked.

He nodded affirmatively and said "Alright, fellas, we're on a mission, y'all ready to ride?"

Freddy unhooked the ropes tying us to the dock. Robbie jumped behind the steering wheel and guided the boat out to the open water. Apparently, our gang was learning how to operate this ocean liner. We were back into our adventure again. The morning sun hinted the day would be hot. We had been into this trip about ten hours and had about eight more to go. We were five people less now; several pounds of fish lighter, bellies filled and ready to get it on.

> "Yo Florida, I see you have some Mother's Finest in your CD holder. Do you mind funk and roll'n for a while?"

> "No I don't mind Gee. I like your choice."

After spending some time talking with Florida I felt more comfortable. His allowing me to drive had also put me more at ease. Throughout the day, I had the opportunity to ask technical questions. I asked Florida about fuel mileage and the number of gallons the boat could carry. I'd hate to think of running out in the middle of the Caribbean Sea.

> "It's necessary when going long distances to carry some extra fuel," he explained. "You don't have gas stations in the middle of the ocean, you know. You just can't get caught without extra go juice. I don't care who you are, you can't do that much rowing."

Traveling during the day was more enjoyable than during the night. The old folks were off the boat, so Florida let the music jam. The field of vision was limitless. It's not like there were historic buildings to look at, no hot mini skirts, either. But being able to see at least prompted us to stay awake, talk. Occasionally, we would see another boat. The ocean is so overwhelmingly vast. The majority of the time, as far as we could see, there was nothing but water.

I recalled to Hakeem, "Remember hearing stories of people being out in the sea for who knows how long, waiting to be rescued?"

"Yeah, you hear about stuff like that every now and then."

"Can you imagine the terror of not knowing how long it would take to be rescued, or even of being attacked by sharks?"

Being in the midst of all this infinity definitely sent a lot of thoughts through my mind. I imagined the loneliness of people who had crossed bodies of water alone in their quest to conquer the ultimate challenge. The little adventures I'd had were miniscule compared to the ocean.

For the next couple of hours, Robbie and Freddy took over the boat as if they owned it. Hakeem and I watched the lines, relaxed, and enjoyed the ride. Florida would go occasionally to check the controls to see if they had the latitude and longitudinal directions correct. Other than that, the boys had everything under control. I was surprised at how enthused they were about operating the thing. It gave them something new to do. It was a unique experience for guys who had never done anything like this. We were all into it. It was still obvious that something was disturbing Florida.

"Slow it down fellas, we got another big one," Florida shouted.

The guys at the controls obeyed the captain's orders. "Yo, Keem, you got this one?" I inquired.

"He's all mine, Homedog!"

It took a couple of minutes, but Hakeem, with Florida's assistance, had everything under control. The fish was within grabbing distance of the boat as Florida and I reached over the side with hooks to haul him up.

"Get him, Gee!" Robbie shouted from the stern as the big

fish flipped on the deck.

"I got him, Dog," I yelled as I made a futile attempt to subdue it.

It was pretty obvious that trying to get this whale into the hull by myself was a little out of my league. It was a little bigger then the amberjack that we had gotten earlier. I bent over and grabbed for him, but he flipped, propelling himself up straight into my face.

"Yuck!" I exclaimed, as the guys laughed.

"Get him, Gee!" I heard someone yell. My timidity was allowing the fish to get the better of me.

"Let me help you, Bro," Florida said, coming to my rescue. Bam! He forcefully stuck the fish as it continued to flop around on the deck. Bam! He got him again. One, two, three more strokes with the steel pipe and that was all he needed. The fish was ready to go in the holding bin. By this time, Robbie had the boat completely stopped and had come down on the deck. Bam, bam, bam! Blood was flying now. Florida angrily kicked the fish as I held the hull door open. It was obvious that the last three stokes weren't necessary. He tossed the steel pipe back into the tool chest.

Hakeem and I looked at each other astonished, at Florida's violent actions.

"All right, Florida, come on with it. Something's bugging the hell out of you, man. What's up?" Robbie queried.

"I'm sorry, man." Florida sat down heavily.

I rebaited the line and tossed it back into the water. The boat was aimlessly floating.

"Talk to me man, you didn't have to kill that fish twice. What's up?"

Florida took a big sigh and slumped on the bench seat for a second. We had been inquiring amongst ourselves as to what was wrong with him. It was that obvious. He had all our attention.

"I'm really worried about the lady we dropped off at Capo," he said finally.

"Oh, okay," Robbie replied.

"That lady is my mother and she didn't look good when we left."

The rest of us sat quietly, listening to Robbie and Florida. "Aw, man, I didn't know that was your mother. You didn't say anything about that."

"Well, I didn't really need to. I just didn't want you guys to think I was charging you and not the other folks that were going with us."

"Man, you crazy. This is your boat and you can do whatever you want. We aren't tripping about who you charge what. We're just happy to be riding with you."

"I appreciate that, Robbie, but I did tell you not to bring any extra stuff with you and they had all those boxes. I didn't want you to think I was trying to pull something over on you."

"Man, you tripping. This is your boat Bro, you can do what you want."

Florida took the liberty to voluntarily explain. "My mother has been living in Miami ever since I was born, but she always called Cuba home. She hasn't been back since."

"Oh, okay."

"My dad owned a fishing boat, too, back in the day, but made his real money smuggling anything from cigars to people. Forty years ago it was easy to do. There wasn't so much technology and control systems to keep up with all the boaters then. My dad met mom in Capo, his regular hangout, which is why I'm so familiar with the place. So when Pop died a few years ago, mom said she always wanted to go back home. She feels like her days are numbered now, and to tell the truth at sixty-five years old, I'm worried about her. She didn't look good, and to tell the truth, I shouldn't have left her."

The boat's canopy shielded us from the sun, which had passed the overhead position, indicating it was early afternoon. My layman's calculations told me we would see land within the next couple of hours. I could have asked, but I didn't want to sound like a little kid again, asking if we were almost there. Our catch of fish was plentiful by now, and I could see that having them was like money. So, since they were available, it made sense to catch them. I felt bad for Florida. Apparently, he was gonna be singing the blues till he could see about his mother. It wasn't as if he could use his cell phone and call. He used his two-way radio to gather information and positions of other boats. Not once did I hear him initiate any conversations. I assumed that since the first part of our journey carried secret cargo he didn't want anyone to know where we were. I was ignorant to the boating business. I thought since leaving Capo we were riding legitimately.

"Yo, Gee, what's up man?" Hakeem shouted over the noise of the boat and sea.

"Just chill'n, man. What's up witchu?"

"Just chill'n, man."

"Just chill'n?"

"Yeah, just chill'n. I know you're looking forward to seeing yo woman. Is she expecting you?"

"Nope."

"You didn't give her the low down?"

"Nope."

"Oh you got it like that... playa, playa."

"Yup. Don't be mad at da playa, be mad at da game."

"I'm gonna be like you when I grow up."

"Maybe, just keep taking notes and you'll be alright."

"Land ahoy!" Robbie yelled.

We stood up and headed towards the bow. "I don't see anything," said Freddy, still standing in his navigator's position.

"Freddy, everybody knows that you couldn't see a stop sign if it was right in front of your face. Wait another hour and you'll see what Robbie's talking about," Hakeem cracked.

We've had a running joke for the longest about Freddy's bad vision.

"I don't know why Gee lets you drive his trucks." Hakeem teased.

"He lets me drive his trucks 'cause I'm good, that's why."

"Another hour and we'll be where we want to be, fellas," Florida said as he tried to muster a smile.

"You know we're going to be partying somewhere tonight," Robbie exclaimed.

"Yup, that's what we came to do." Hakeem said. "Four days of fine, sexy talking honeys. I just love the way they talk. What about you, Florida? You know you like them pretty, brown skinned thangs,"

"Hey, man, I'd be lying if I said I didn't. Where you guys gonna be staying? I got a hook up with a hotel that has a restaurant. I can make a deal with the fish for all us if you want."

"Yo, Bro, you talking about that place you and I partied at with those ladies?" Robbie asked.

"Yeah, that's right Robbie, you know the place."

"Hey, man, that's the perfect place, nice rooms and right in the middle of everything. You really know how to work them fish."

"Like I said, they're just as good as money sometimes. Besides, what hotel manager with a restaurant can turn down two hundred pounds of fish. Why buy it when most likely his place is not full. It doesn't cost him a thing for us to use a room for a couple of days. His only problem might be a place to keep that much fish. I imagine there's enough to take home for his family, too. Yep, having fresh fish is just like having money."

"Yo, Florida, you don't mind if I take some to my girl's house do you?" I asked.

"No Gee, there's more than enough here man, take what you want."

"Thanks man you my nig..." I caught myself forgetting that Florida was white.

Florida smiled as he caught my near slip of the tongue. "You can use one of the coolers. Just don't forget to bring it back."

"That'll work."

"Yo, Florida," Freddy interjected, "I remember seeing fishing boats off shore when we were on the beach. I guess you really could save on docking fees by just anchoring in the water, couldn't you?"

"I've always felt it was a pain in the butt to make a special trip to an immigration port, and pay the entry fees, when my destination is miles away somewhere else, Florida explained. "Yes, Freddy, we can park this thing anywhere as long as there's water. You learn quickly, I'mma keep you around for a while." Florida responded in a seemingly natural, black dialect. If he had ended his sentence with 'my nigga,' no one would have said a word.

Freddy continued, "I'm just wondering how you get back and forth to the boat."

"That's not so hard; you just flag down a smaller boat and give'm a few bucks. When we get to shore we can find somebody to act as a taxi every time we want to go back and forth. Besides, it pays to have somebody watch the boat."

"And you pay with fish?"

"Like I said Freddy, you learn quickly. I might keep you around a while."

We Made It

Chapter 16

Land was well within sight by now. Even blind Freddy could pick out the familiar places. "Yo, fellas, there's the Treehouse. You can see all six miles of Negril's beach."

Robbie was still at the wheel as Florida directed him to go a little closer to shore and further down towards the cliff area. "We have to keep an eye on this depth meter so we don't bottom out."

I could see some of the familiar glass bottom boats docked near the hotels. The first time I went to Jamaica, I did the tourist thing and went out on one. They're nice for what they do; if you want to snorkel, they will take you out to see some of the reefs. When we found a good stopping spot, we caught the attention of one of these boats. It didn't take long for the driver to come out to where we were.

I guessed it was about six o'clock. The sun heading toward the horizon made a perfect postcard picture. The heat of the day was over and I was glad to be getting the heck off the boat. Partly glad to have made it all the way with no dilemmas and also glad not to have gotten sick. A native tongue greeted us as he pulled alongside. "Good afternoon, gentlemen, how can I be of assistance?"

I instantly recognized my young friend Robert from the Treehouse. "Yeah, I need a jogging partner in the morning, how many miles you good for?" I turned my head so he couldn't see my face.

"You can't fool me, Mr. Gee. Me recognize dat bald head anywhere. What's up?" Robert tossed a rope to Florida to pull our boats closer together.

"Robert! What's up man?"

"Respect, Mon, good to see you again."

"Yo, fellas, this is my buddy Robert, you might remember him from the time we all stayed at the Treehouse." Everybody greeted our new chauffeur. "Hey, man, looks like I got some business for you."

The boats were in position now to allow us to board Robert's. Florida anchored his and prepared to exit.

"Well, Gee, if you remember, me told you about me plan to do dis. Me found da window of opportunity and when da window is open you have to move before it close." We shook hands and hugged like Brothas do. A familiar smell hit me in the face.

"Robert... man, it's good to see you. I'm so proud of you man, you did exactly like you said you were gonna do. Shoot I can ask you for some money now."

"Oh, no it's not like dat yet! Give me a minute or two more and me see den."

Everybody had climbed aboard now and found a seat. Florida was the last. As he was still standing, I introduced him. "Robert this is our Captain Florida."

"Pleased to meet you, Robert."

"Yeah, mon."

"There's a few things I'm gonna need you to do for me," Florida began.

"No problem, Mon, If you be a friend of Mr. Gee, den you be a friend of mine."

"First of all I got a bunch of fish to get rid of, like this evening cause they're not on ice. So, if you can direct me to a hotel with a restaurant, then we'll be in business."

Robert answered, "If you take care of me den me take care of you. But me know already if you wit me friend Gee, you a good Mon too. Me know exactly were to take you, Mon, we can go dere right now if you want."

I looked at Florida and he agreed that was what we wanted. "Robert, I'm proud of you man." I gave him a soul shake again without the hug.

We took a five-minute ride to a spot Robert had in mind. Robert and Florida got their feet wet as the boat could only get so far on the beach. They headed toward the hotel to transact business. Freddy spoke up as he saw several people sunbathing on the hotel's property. "I don't know about y'all, but I hope like hell they can work out a deal for us to stay here."

"I'm ready to get this party started now," Robbie replied.

One of the native beach hustlers approached. "What's up? You need anyting to smoke? Me got what you need."

"Yo, man, let me see what you got," Robbie answered.

The dread-locked man dressed in shorts waded out five feet in the water and discretely opened his bag to show us what he had. He suspiciously looked around and said, "Me give you a good price, Mon, what's up?"

Robbie said, "I tell you what man, as soon as we get settled, I'm gonna look you up. We're just getting here but I could use a little of that."

"Yah Mon, how bout me meet you here in about an hour. Me be walking on de beach, is dat cool wit you?"

"Yeah, that's cool with me. I'll see you in about an hour."

Florida and Robert came briskly walking back. Florida was rubbing his hands together with a smile on his face. It was good to see him smile again. "We got two bedrooms for the next three days with access to the breakfast buffet. And my boat is within walking distance too? I'm happy."

We headed back to the boat to get our bags and unload the fish. It had been a long trip. We had left Miami almost twenty-four hours ago. I got a little sleep, but not much, and not like I was in my own bed. I was energized, like everyone else by the novelty of what we had done; of course, it was nothing new to Florida. This was something I could tell my grandchildren about. This even ranks right up there with parachuting. This was one of those things that you can say you did and appreciate having the nerve. Not just everybody could do it. We did it and we were all excited. I liked this adventure. I was ready to head toward my second home now.

Reunited

Chapter 17

The beach hotel the gang was staying at was nice. They were all hyped and talking about partying already. The location was good, one side on the beach, the other fronting the road. It was getting dark now. I walked through the courtyard to the roadside. It took a little while to flag down a route taxi that could accommodate my cooler of about thirty pounds of fish. From there, the driver took me to the central cabstand to catch another heading to Little London. It was going to cost me twice the fare of seventy-five cents because of the cooler, which was fine with me. I was tired and just ready to get to Jacy's. The trip took about twenty minutes. Mr. Weber was sitting on the porch steps.

"Hey, Gee."

"Hello Mr. Weber, how are you?"

"Fine, Mon, good to see you. How's everyting?"

We shook hands. I could feel the years of hard living in the texture of his hand. "I don't have any complaints Mr. Weber, none at all."

After carrying my bag up to the house, I returned to the street to get the cooler full of fish. I brought it over to where he was sitting and opened it to show him my prize.

"Nice, Mon, you need me to clean dem for you?" His toothless, broad smile showed his approval.

By my calculations, Jacy had gotten home an hour or so ago. "Is Jacy home yet?"

"Yah Mon, she here but she's a bit busy."

"Let me go say hello to her, and then I'll help you clean the fish." I started towards the outside entrance to Jacy's room .

"No, Mon, we take care of de fish now," Mr. Weber directed. "Come put de bag here." He pointed to a spot beside his seat. "Come, Mon." He stood now, waiting for me to follow.

He led me around back of the little wooden house to an area that was appropriate to make a mess cleaning fish. From his dilapidated shed, he retrieved the tools that we needed. Cleaning fish right about now was the furthest thing from my mind. I'd been going, although leisurely at times on the boat, for about twenty-four hours. I was beat, and in such desperate need of a shower that I would have made my buddy Robert take a step backward, had he gotten a whiff of me. Now I'm cleaning fish, scales flying everywhere. And then, here come the flies.

"Nice fish, Gee."

"Uh huh." Unfortunately, the flies didn't have to come far, because even though Jacy had installed an indoor bathroom in her bedroom, the outhouse still was being used. I wondered if these big, fat, nasty flies had been in the outhouse? Probably. Now, as if the flies weren't bad enough, the mosquitoes started buzzing around my head. I couldn't really swat them because my hands were full of fish gunk.

"No, Gee, don't cut off de head Mon," Mr. Weber's voice broke into my misery.

Outhouse flies flying, mosquitoes skeet'n, and I couldn't swat anything 'cause I got fish gunk all over my hands. Mr. Weber was just cleaning like nothing was happening. Talking about, "don't cut off de head."

"Sorry, Mr. Weber, I forgot that you like the head." We had been cleaning about fifteen minutes. Mr. Weber cleaned two fish to my one. I endured about two more fish and just couldn't take anymore. I turned and spit an imaginary fish scale out of my mouth. I saw the familiar outdoor shower that I'd used before the indoor facilities had been installed. Finally, my contortionist imitation - rubbing my chin on my shoulder, elbow on top of my head, standing on one foot and scratching my left kneecap with my right calf - tipped Mr. Weber off that I was uncomfortable.

"You okay, Gee?"

"Yo, Mr. Weber, I think I hear the shower over there calling me.

"Eh?"

Not taking the time to explain, I tossed my last half-cleaned fish back into the cooler. I flung my hands free of all the fish gunk possible, did the heal toe/heal toe step out of my sneakers, and headed towards the shower. It wasn't so odd to take a shower with clothes on because that's how they get washed sometimes. It was good that I had shorts on, but bad because the mosquitoes had taken advantage of it. The water was cold but I didn't care; it was an escape from the attack bugs. A bar of soap in its familiar place made my day.

"All of a sudden, I heard a familiar voice screeching, "Gee! Gee!" Jacy came running in my direction. I turned off the shower and caught her in mid-air.

"Baby, baby, baby, I'm soaking wet."

"I don't care." She kissed me as her legs wrapped around me to keep her off the ground.

"Hey, Baby, how are you?"

"Hey, Baby. Dere's a strange bag on me porch. Me hoped it belonged to you.

"Hey, Baby."

"Me look for Daddy and see him cleaning fish. Me wonder who bring dem."

"Hey, Baby. You surprised to see me?"

"Yes, what you bring me?"

"What did I bring you? I brought you me, what else you want?"

"Well, you could've brought me a pretty dress, or maybe perfume."

"Oh, I see, I guess I have to leave if I didn't bring you anything?"

"No, Mon, just kidding. Me glad just to have you and your

bald head." She kissed me again.

"Girl, if you don't get down you gonna break my back."

"Oh your back gonna get broke all right, but not in dis shower."

"Ah ha, you missed me, didn't you?"

"Yup."

"It was okay to come unannounced?"

"Yup, let me get you a towel, me soon come."

Just as quickly as she came, she left and was back drying me off.

"Thank you, dear, you're so wonderful. You're the most wonderfulest girl I ever met."

"Yeah, yeah, me bet you tell dat to all dem American girls dat be trying to get you, Gee."

"Huh? What you talking about, girl, nobody wants me but you."

"Come, Gee, let's go in de house."

We could have walked in the back door, but Mr. Weber and the flies made us take a detour. I picked up my shoes along the way to the front. Two mysterious looking, elderly ladies stood quietly in the darkness of the front yard. It appeared that they were waiting for someone to come pick them up. My wetness was concealed by the darkness.

"Goodnight again, ladies." Jacy called out.

They acknowledged with hand gestures. I grabbed my bag and left my shoes at the door. Entering the front door, I saw that candles had been burning on the kitchen table. Incense smoke wafted through the air. The atmosphere within the house was unfamiliar to me. Jacy and I sometimes burned candles and incense in the bedroom, but that was to enhance our romance. I headed toward my familiar spot in her room to put my bag down and finish making myself at home.

"Gee, me make you some of de fish if you want?" Jacy called to me from the other room.

"Girl, you all right with me. You know I love the way you fix fish. I came all the way here just for that. Where's Mika?"

"Eh?"

"I said, where's Mika," I spoke up a little louder.

"She's at me sister's house. Me have a meeting dis evening so she went dere. She be back tomorrow."

"Okay. She been doing all right?" I asked, walking back out to the living area.

"Yes, Gee. What you want wit de fish?"

"Baby, anything you fix is fine with me. You know that."

I sat on the long ago worn out sofa, adjusted the TV, and was out like a light.

The aroma of Jamaican authentically prepared fish awakened me. The weight of the plate on my lap slowly brought me back to my senses. She sat beside me as I ate, watching every move I made, like a little girl watching her daddy shave for the first time. I was back in another world now, a peaceful place. Far removed from customers, employees, and trucks. I savored each bite, wishing that I could get such loving service at home. Mr. Weber gave us our space. Jacy gave me all her attention.

"Tank you for de present, Gee. You just coming to see me is better den any dress or perfume dat you could buy," she said lovingly caressing the back of my head.

"After being on that boat all night and day, the closer I got to your house, the more excited I got. I was like a little puppy dog ready to pee on myself." Jacy laughed, showing her pretty white teeth.

"Me want you to lay your bald head on me stomach tonight?" I dropped a forkful of fish back onto the plate. She picked it up and put it in my mouth for me.

"I like it when you feed me."

Jacy leaned close to my ear. "Me like it when you make love to me."

"Girl, let me put this fish down right now." I started to get up.

"No, Mon, finish de food," Jacy laughed. "Me enjoy watching you eat. Besides, you gonna need de energy for tonight and in de morning."

"You gotta go to work in the morning?"

"Yup."

"Here, Baby, help me eat this. You know you always give me too much food." I started to feed her.

"Where you get dis fish?"

"We caught it on the boat as we were coming."

"Yeah?"

"You should have seen all the fish we had. The guys took them to a hotel and traded for their stay. We had quite a bit."

"How dey know to do dat?"

"The guy that owns the boat is pretty smart. He knows his business well. Girl, you ought to see that boat."

"Yeah, you take me dere?"

"Sure. When we came in today, a Jamaican guy I remember from one of the hotels has a boat of his own now. We happened to run into him and he helped us out."

"Oh, okay."

"Girl, I don't know what I like most, you or your cooking."

"Tank you Gee, me glad you like it. Dere's more if you want."

"I can't eat another bite."

"Oh, yes you can."

"Oh, no I can't."

"Me no talk'n about more food Mon. Come." Jacy took the plate to the kitchen and said, "Me meet you in de room."

I remember hearing her in the shower. The next thing I remember hearing was the clamor of some road beaten vehicles and chickens.

Big Disappointment

Chapter 18

"Good morning, sir. Did you sleep well?"

"Hey, Baby." It took me a minute to realize that I wasn't in my own bed. "I fell asleep on you last night. I'm sorry."

"Oh, don't worry, you did what you were supposed to do and as well as usual. How old did you say you were?"

"I hate to tell you this, but I don't remember anything."

"Yeah, right."

"Really I don't. Evidently the trip really wore me out. Sorry, I'll make it up to you tonight, Baby."

"Gee, if we do noting more while you're here, me be fine."

"It sounds like you took advantage of me last night."

"Yup, sure did."

"What time is it?"

"Tis six-tirty."

"You want me to go to work with you and hang around for a while?"

"Yes, because it's been so long since me see you, me want you to be close in case me need a kiss or sump'n."

"Okay, Baby. I can go to the hotel where the guys are, then come back when you get off."

Jacy had some tea and fruit sitting on the dresser. "Looks like you brought breakfast already. I might keep you. You know that?"

"Yup. Me hope so," she replied, zipping up her skirt.

Watching Jacy get dressed aroused me. "Yo, you got a minute?"

"Eh?"

"Come back and lie down for a little while."

"No, Mon, me got to go, and if you're going you'd better get up, too."

I got up making sure she saw my buddy at attention. She laughed. "You're bad, you know dat."

"What? What you talking about?"

"You know what me talk'n about."

We stood out front of the house waiting for a taxi. It was a beautiful day. Waking up with my sweetheart was a joy. I had been anxious to be right here doing exactly this ever since the gang decided to accept Florida's invitation.

"What you going to do today, Gee?"

"Think about you all day."

"No, Mon, really." A taxi came and we piled in. It was tight, but with my arm around her shoulders and legs crossed, we made it.

"Well, if it's all right with you I'll hang around the office for a little while and give the guys a chance to wake up. They probably stayed up later than I did." We chatted and giggled the twenty-minute ride to the central cabstand. It was obvious that we were glad to see each other. After unfolding my body from the cab, I had to loosen up for a second.

"What's the matter," Jacy asked. "You getting old?"

"That's not what you said last night."

"Ah ha! Me knocked you out last night; you don't remember anyting me said."

"Oh, is that right?"

"Yup." We walked hand-in-hand the two blocks to her office. Her never-ending smile told me she was happy. She had the key to open the place for business. I sat around for a couple of hours, reading anything that

123

I could find. We talked when she got a break from customers and just enjoyed the opportunity to hang out and be together. It had been six months since I had seen her, and we both were as giddy as high school kids. Guessing that the guys were up and moving around, I decided to go to the hotel. Even if I couldn't find them, I could just hang out on the beach. I knew it was a good walk, and with the afternoon sun approaching, I thought by the time I got there I'd be ready to jump in the water. As I approached their room, I could see Freddy sitting at the table on the verandah, and Hakeem lounging in a hammock.

"Yo, fellas, what's up?"

"You know what it is, Gee, back in paradise again, man, and I ain't even mad," Hakeem replied.

"I feel you, Bro. I almost expected to see you guys still in bed. Y'all must have crashed last night instead of hitting the beach parties."

Freddy spoke up, "Man, after that long-ass boat ride, I hit the shower and fell out. I wasn't thinking about any parties."

"Have you guys hit that breakfast buffet yet?"

"Yup," they answered, at the same time.

I detected a sullen atmosphere.

"You have the royal treatment last night, Gee?" Hakem asked.

"Yup, after I fought with fish, flies, and mosquitoes, my baby took good care of me. Fired me some fish up, rice and peas, a little salad and a Red Stripe and I don't remember anything else."

"Hey, well check this out," Freddy said. "Florida called this morning to check on his mom and it didn't sound too good."

"Aw, man."

"Says he might have to go back to Capo immediately."

"Aw, man!" My voice rose this time.

"Yup," Hakeem replied.

"Well, that definitely throws a different light on the subject." Stunned, I sat at the table looking in the direction of the beach. "Where's Florida now?"

"Him and Robbie took off somewhere, said they were going to get something to eat."

We sat in silence for a moment.

"Wait a minute, we get to hit the breakfast buffet here for free, which was part of the deal, you know. Why would they go buy the exact same kind of food when we can get it free, especially as cheap as Robbie is?"

"Gee, that's exactly the same thing Freddy and I were talking about just before you came. Those two are starting to trip me out."

"What you mean, Hak?"

"I don't know man, they just too chummy-chummy for me."

"Florida can go back to Capo if he wants, they got flights heading out of here everyday, fellas," Freddy suggested.

"Freddy, you a buckethead." I reprimanded. "Yeah, they got flights but we can't get on them. We're here illegally. We didn't go through any immigration port when we came. We brought our passports, but they aren't gonna do us any good."

"Wonder what they'd do if we tried to catch a flight?" Hakeem asked.

"I don't know, but to avoid a bunch of turmoil we might as well just rack this up to the game and head back if Florida decides to split," I replied. "Jacy is not going to be too happy if I have to leave unexpectedly."

"Gee and his women," Freddy chuckled."

"Freddy, at least I got some women."

"I got some women, too, I just keep 'em at a distance."

"That's 'cause you be chewing on yo socks. I told you to stop. Well look, I'm gonna go cool out in the water and check out one of the gazebos on the beach. I'll yell atcha when I yell atcha."

There was plenty of activity on the beach. There were plenty of bikinis, the hotel was having two for one drinks between one and four, the music was kicking, and the place was live. Jumping in the water was right on time. After staying in it long enough to cool down from the day's heat, I found a comfortable spot to take in the sights. My body's clock was still off and demanded sleep that came very quickly.

Waking with a startle, I panicked when I realized where I was, and that I had to keep up with the time. "Ma'am, do you have the time?" I asked the first person I saw.

"Depends on what you have in mind." Some women should just forget about wearing a two-piece bathing suit, like someone wanted to see her big booty.

"Sorry, I mean do you have the time of day, Ma'am?"

Her disposition changed when she realized I wouldn't reciprocate her flirting. She looked at her watch and said bluntly, "It's five-thirty."

I realized I had slept longer than I should've, got my self together, and took a taxi back to Jacy's job.

"Hey, Pretty," I spoke to her through the glass partition.

"Wait a minute, me soon come." She shuffled some papers for a minute before coming from behind the locked door. "Me done for de day. De oder girls will lock up. What we gonna get into?"

"Remember I was going to show you the boat that brought us here. Interested?"

"Sure, why not? As long as I'm wit you Gee, I don't care what we do."

We flagged down a taxi and made the mile ride. We cut through one of the hotels to the beach where I thought the boat was. It was in sight, but I hadn't really judged its position correctly. So we took off our shoes and had our little romantic walk in the water hand-in-hand. We sat talking in the shade waiting for someone to appear with a boat to give us the short shuttle ride.

"If me had me bating suit we could go for a swim, Gee."

"Well, since I've had my swim already, you can borrow mine if you want."

"No, me don't think so."

Within fifteen minutes, I could see Robert coming back in with some tourists on board. When he was done unloading, I asked him for a ride out to Florida's boat.

"Good afternoon, Lady J. It's good to see you again."
Robert spoke to Jacy.

"Hello, Robert, you see dat, dreams really do come true."

"Yes, Ma'am, dat's why me dream more often now."

Noticing that they were familiar with each other I just listened. Negril being rather small and Jacy working in a public place made sense that they might know each other. Then they started speaking a patois that left me in the dark. Robert tied us to Florida's boat and helped Jacy make the transition.

"Tank you," she said as she stepped on. She was amazed that it was so big. I showed her around, taking her upstairs and down to the bedrooms, as Robert waited. I didn't want to keep my old friend from making his money, so we soon headed back to shore. They started up their conversation again, and still, I had no clue what they were talking about.

"Thanks, Robert," I said. "Don't work too hard." We shook hands, concealing the couple of bucks I gave him.

"Respect, Mon."

It was about seven-thirty when we arrived home. Mika was there when we arrived.

"Hey, Mr. Gee, what you bring me dis time?"

"Hey, girl, I got a booty whooping in my pocket if you haven't been doing your homework and leaving those boys alone. What's his name anyway"?

"What who name, Gee?"

"Your boyfriend?"

"Me no have no boyfriend, Mon, why you say dat?"

"That's not what Jacy has been telling me."

"Ooh, Auntie J, what you tell him?"

"Me no tell him noting, Mika. He making it up."

I handed her a twenty-dollar bill as we went into Jacy's room. "Here, Mika, and don't spend it all in one place."

"Tank you, Mr. Gee."

"You know why me love you, Gee? Because you are a good Mon." Jacy stopped me in the middle of her crowded room and looked me straight in the eyes. "That was very nice of you to do dat for Mika. Why you have to live over dere and me live over here? Me ask dat question all de time, but me no know de answer. Me question de moon and stars and still me no know. Me try to be patient, Gee. Me ask Jah when me blessing come. But him say dat everyting no come when we want it. If Jah's blessing was for you to show up at me step unexpectedly, den I accept. Tis bad for me to want more, Gee? Me must be patient but it's very hard. Sometime me tink me hope against hope, wanting to be your wife so."

"Jacy, ever since I have known you, it has been a pleasure. I have always appreciated you and your family, and especially the opportunity to come and go as I please. Don't think that there is not a special place in my heart for you." The phone rang but Jacy refused to answer it. She looked at it in disgust, as if it were an annoyance. She hugged me tighter and returned her eyes to mine as if to continue our conversation.

"Telephone," Mika called through the bedroom door.

"Me busy, Mika, take a message, please."

"It not for you, it for Mr. Gee."

"I gave the guys your number, Baby, in case they needed to get ahold of me." I had to pry myself from Jacy's grip. She was holding me as if she didn't want me to answer the call.

"Gee!"

I took a step toward the phone as she grabbed me again. It was within arm's length now. "Hello, hey Hakeem. What's up?" I listened without saying a word for about fifteen seconds. Then another ten. "And he can't wait till tomorrow?" Jacy's eyes welled up as if she could hear every word. "All right... all right... Where are you at now? Okay I'm heading that way now, I'll meet you at the hotel. Bye."

"Gee, what de problem?" She asked brokenly, unable to hold back the tears.

"The guy that owns the boat has to leave. His mother is very ill."

"No, Gee!"

"Yes, Baby, when we dropped her and some others off in Cuba, she collapsed on the dock. I thought she was just overwhelmed with joy to be back home. Apparently, there was more to it than that."

"Gee, you can't leave. You just got here."

"I know, Baby, but it's out of my control."

"Please, don't leave." Jacy was sobbing uncontrollably now. I had trouble understanding what she was saying.

"I'm sorry, Baby." A few seconds passed before she tried to speak again.

"You can stay, let de Mon and de guys go by demsef." Unable to hold her limp body up I let her slowly sink to the floor. Jacy's sobs turned into the wailing of a broken heart. If Mr. Weber and Mika had been within earshot, I'm sure they would have been knocking on the door to see what the problem was. "Him no need you to operate de boat," she cried piteously.

I went to the bathroom to get tissue, returned and sat on the floor, holding her as tightly as I could.

> "Baby, I think I'm gonna have a problem if I try to catch a flight out later. We didn't come through Customs, so the government doesn't even know we're here."

I had never seen Jacy so emotional. We had both cried when I'd previously left, not knowing when I'd be back. With a little joking and stroking, I'd always managed to bring a smile back to her face. This time was different. I could feel her anguish coming from deep within. Minutes passed as a river of tears fell. She finally gathered herself enough to talk.

> "Gee, ask de boatman if him got anyting from him mother."

I was puzzled by her inquiry. "What?"

> "Go to de man and see if him got a special rosary dat him carry for her. Gee, him wallet probably got a picture of her too." She started crying again. "Yes Gee, you ask him and bring it to me. Me bring de ladies over and pray special prayers over it and she get better."

> "Jacy."

> "Gee, me no tell you everyting, but me can help him mother. Me promise."

I recalled the time I first met Jacy. She never did tell me what she did to bring that big chill over me when she touched me on my shoulder. That puzzled me for the longest. Freddy even commented about it later. To add to Jacy's astonishing feats, I was still flabbergasted that she'd dreamed about the boat trip immediately before it happened. Maybe she did have something going on that I couldn't figure out. And what about the old ladies, candles, and incense yesterday? As long as I have been in this world, I know darn well that I have good sense. Now Jacy is telling me to ask Florida if she and some old ladies can pray over some articles to make his mother feel better. I didn't feel comfortable approaching Florida like that, especially since he was already down and out, worried sick about his mother's condition. He'd think I was crazy. Shoot, I'd think I was crazy.

"Baby, I hate to go worse than you hate for me to go. I didn't come all this way to just turn around and go right back. Hakeem said they were waiting on me and would be leaving as soon as I got there. I'll tell you what, Baby, if I promise to come back as soon as I can, would that make you feel better?"

"Okay, Gee." There was disappointment in her voice.

"As soon as I get home I'll call you and tell you when my schedule will allow me to come back."

"Okay, Gee."

I picked up the bag of the few items I'd brought.

"When you get yourself together, tell your Dad and Mika why I had to leave so abruptly."

We walked to the door. I could feel her broken heart as I gave her one last hug. Trying my best to keep myself together, I kissed her passionately, her lips moistened by streams of tears. As I closed the door behind me, I could hear the excruciating wails of her breaking down again.

Gotta Go

Chapter 19

R obbie, the first one I saw as I approached the hotel, was outside smoking a joint. "Yo Reefer Madness, where you been all day?" I called out.

"Damn, man, you scared me sneaking up on me like that."

"How was I sneaking up on you, man? You need to be paying attention to your surroundings. If I'd been a cop, I doubt if you'd be getting on a boat anytime soon. Like I said, what you been doing all day?"

"Trying to keep an eye on Florida. You know he has been singing the blues all day trying to find out about his mom."

"Man, I be wondering about you and yo boy." He choked as he took another hit. "That stuff gonna kill you boy and make you stupid."

"What you mean 'wondering about me and my boy?'"

"I'm trying to figure out why y'all went out to find something to eat when the deal at the hotel was to have free breakfast."

"No, man, Florida and me went to look up some ladies we had met here before."

"See that's what I'm talking about, Robbie. Florida is supposed to be so worried about his mom and you guys are out chasing poonanny. That doesn't make any sense to me. I guess he don't be getting any back in the States, huh?" Robbie was trying to talk and smoke, but gagged instead. "Man, that stuff done made you stupid already."

"Like you have never smoked no reefer while listening to Rick James."

"I don't hear any Rick James playing now. I'm ready to go if we gonna go." I left Robbie to his choking and smoking and went to the room.

Florida was on the phone sitting at the kitchen table. As I walked in, Freddy gave me a look of super disgust. "Win a few, lose a few, Gee."

"Sometimes it's like that Freddy. Y'all 'bout ready to ride?"

"Yeah, I'm just waiting on everybody else. Hakeem is in the bathroom. After killing the free breakfast thing this morning, he's been running to the john all day."

When Florida saw that I had finally arrived, he got off the phone and came into the room. "I'm sorry about the unforeseen turn of events, Gee." He looked awfully sullen. I felt his apology was genuine. We all had seen his mom fall out. So we knew she was not feeling well. I couldn't imagine that he would come this far to turn around and go back on a humbug. We were all prepared to have fun and relax for a few days. In the end, we could still say that we had the chance to ride a boat across the Caribbean Sea. "Whenever you guys get the chance, you got my boat and me, whenever. That's the least I can do for you guys."

Freddy yelled at Hakeem through the bathroom door. "Yo, Homedog, I know yo booty raw from wiping all day, but hit dat badboy one more time and let's ride. We're waiting on you."

"All right, give me a minute."

"I got Robert on standby, fellas, I'm heading down that way." Florida said as he and Robbie started walking towards the water taxi.

"Yo, Freddy, what do I have to do to make a call on this phone real quick?" I asked hurriedly.

"Just dial 'O' and the operator will ask you for the number you want to call."

I followed his instruction and waited a second. "Hey, Mika, this is Gee, may I speak to Jacy please?"

"Eh?"

"Is Jacy there?"

"No, Gee, me thought she left wit you."

"Huh?"

"Me be in her room for de last hour watching TV. She not here, Mon."

"Mika, Jacy is not with me. Stop playing and put Jacy on the phone."

"Gee, me swear she not here."

The phone was silent for a few seconds. I was expecting Mika to say she was joking.

"Okay, Baby, please tell her I called." I said finally.

"Okay."

"You promise to tell her?"

"Yeah, Mon, me promise."

"Thank you, sweetheart. I'll talk to you later."

Since I had to leave Jamaica like this, I regretted coming. What a drag to leave Jacy under such circumstances. Poor girl was acting like she was on her last leg. I would have stopped and gone back to her rescue if I had the opportunity, but I couldn't. If it were up to me, I would have done anything to console her. My heart was breaking just because Jacy was so disappointed. The only way I thought to make up for something that I had no control over, was to come back as soon as I could. That's what I decided to do, and with that pretty dress she wanted. That girl was about to die and now that she wasn't at home, I worried that she might hurt herself. Adventure my booty, I should have kept it at home.

"Yo, fellas, let's get out of here." The three of us started walking.

My buddy Robert was unusually quiet as he taxied us toward

Florida's big boat. I knew that he got up early to start his day. It was about eleven o'clock and I imagined he was tired. We grabbed our bags and I was the last to exit his boat. As we shook hands, he hugged me and whispered in my ear, "Be careful, Mon." He gave me cause to be concerned not by what he said, but by the way he looked at me when he said it. I felt like he wanted to tell me something else. It took me a second to comprehend his attempted secret message, but by that time I had one foot in the big boat, and for the sake of balance, I was committed to follow immediately with the other.

"Respect, Mon."

"Later, Robert," I replied as everyone got busy untying the ropes and pulling the anchor.

The moonlit sky presented another postcard setting. For me, it was all for naught; I couldn't appreciate its radiance. We all were in position as we headed out to sea — Florida navigating directions, Robbie playing Captain again. I just realized that I had not eaten anything all day except for the little Jacy fixed that morning. The changes that I had seen Jacy go through had taken away any concern for food. I figured it was all for the better. At least I wouldn't have to worry about getting seasick from too much on my stomach. Unfortunately, I had gotten a long nap that afternoon and wouldn't be able to make my body go to sleep. Freddy, Hakeem, and I talked about nothing for a while as we got used to the noise of the boat and waves. Before we knew it, a couple of hours had gone by.

Florida suggested that we put out the fishing lines. "It's nothing new, fellas, a fishing boat is worthless without any fish." This reminded me that fish were like money and could be used to barter. I almost felt like asking Florida if he could trade this next load for something that would compensate for a trip made in vain. I had to ask for the Lord's forgiveness for even letting that thought come into my head. If it had been my mother, I would have done exactly what Florida was doing. As a matter of fact, there is nothing more important than the health and welfare of our loved ones. Whatever Florida could do to help his mother regain her health, he ought to do it. There was no use in singing the blues about having to cut short our trip. It was something that had to be done. My concern was for Jacy's welfare. Until I heard from her, I'd be concerned. Like the song says "It's just one of them days." My mind was running now, thinking to myself, pumping me up, "Yo, Gee, you got to take the bitter with the sweet. You win a few, you lose a few. At least you're in the game."

Florida knew what he was doing; before long we were catching fish. This gave us something to do. Again, we had no scenery to admire, only darkness. Our navigator kept us on course and another hour went by. The ocean's wet air had everyone in jackets. We'd change seats, walk around the deck a little, and another hour went by. By now even Hakeem was honing his skills at the wheel, and another hour went by. Robbie said he was sleepy and went downstairs to lie down. He immediately ran back up.

"Yo, Gee, come here!" Robbie called out, as if there was a problem.

I was surprised to hear so much urgency in his tone. I headed down to the sleeping quarters. "What's up, man?" Robbie grabbed me by the arm, leading me to a small space on the floor, between the bed and the wall. Jacy sat there wrapped in bed linen looking at us looking at her.

Stunned silence seized the atmosphere; even the sound of the boat and ocean were gone. I managed to walk over and help her up. No one spoke. I hugged Jacy with an effort to relieve any discomfort she may have felt. I stroked her body trying to alleviate any pains. I kissed her forehead to eradicate any stress and fear. Still no one said a word. Recalling the torment that she had expressed as I was leaving, I wanted to heal the broken heart that pressed against my chest. I kissed her forehead to tell her that I loved her and understood why she did what she did. Seeing her relieved my worry that she might not be okay.

"Are you okay?" I asked.

"Yes. Me butt not doing too good, it hurt from sitting so long."

I started massaging her rear and Robbie exited the room. He had nothing to do but deliver the news to the others of our unexpected passenger. The boat stopped it's forward motion and shortly afterward, everyone appeared. I felt like an item on display as the group looked in disbelief, Jacy still in the shelter of my arms.

136

Nobody said a word. Florida retreated back to the helm to resume his duties.

Freddy spoke up softly, "Jacy, how you doing, girl? I haven't seen you in a month of Sundays."

"Eh?" She looked at me asking, "what him mean by dat?"

"He said he hasn't seen you in a long time." Everyone went back to doing whatever they were doing.

I didn't know what to think, much less say. Jacy asked, "You fretting wit me, Gee?"

Thinking that our dilemma had now been compounded, I replied, "No, Baby, I'm glad to see that you're all right. You had me worried that you may have done something stupid." My worry was justifiable because this was one of those things that might be considered stupid. Stupid because her family didn't know where she was. Stupid because she hadn't made preparations to leave her job. Stupid because I was responsible for her now and I had not made any preparations for it, no papers, no plans, no nothing. We sat down on the bed holding hands. I placed the bed linen back around her. Florida reappeared.

The only thing I could say was that I was sorry for our unexpected visitor. He looked past me and said, "So, this is Lady J? I'm so glad you're here, Ma'am." This was the second time in as many days that someone referred to her as 'Lady J.' Robert had used it and now Florida. It puzzled me that I had never heard anyone call her that before.

I was totally surprised at his greeting. I had no idea what route his reaction was going to take.

"Robert told me that he brought a special woman to my boat yesterday."

"Yes, me come to de boat yesterday, but only because Gee wanted to show me around."

Listening to their conversation stunned me into silence again. Robert had called her 'special.'

"Lady J, it is a blessing to say the least that I have this opportunity to meet you." Florida kneeled at her feet and took her hand. "I'm sure you know why we had to discontinue our trip. I am worried sick that my mother may be on her deathbed as we speak."

"Yes, me know dat you cut short yo time on de island."

"Since my father's unexpected death, I have been my mother's only provider. His wish was that she could return to live her last days in her homeland of Cuba. I think the excitement of returning was too much for her heart. If I may beg you to help her, if I may ask you to call upon your authority and assist her in any way possible, I will forever be in your debt. I know I could never repay you a fair wage, but my prayer is that you can do something for her. Please, Lady J."

"Me see in your eye dat you be like Gee, a good Mon. Me do anyting for him and Jah permitting, me do what me can for yo Mudda."

Robbie's shout of "Land ahoy" was followed by the sun peaking over the horizon. It had taken eight hours for us to make the second half of our original trip, and the same to return. Florida, Jacy, and I walked upstairs to the deck. I watched in amusement at Jacy's reaction to the activity around her. The guys had been doing their duties as fishermen. Jacy covered her mouth in surprise as she saw the full fish bin. I hugged her close to me. It was a relief to know that she was okay. To see and touch her reassured me of that.

"Have I told you lately that I love you?" I whispered in her ear.

"Yup, all de time," she replied.

"Well, I'm gonna tell you again because I do. I love you Baby."

"Me love you too Gee."

I again became aware of the noise of the boat, and heard the waves crashing against the sides. I pinched myself to verify that all my senses had fully returned.

Risking Paradise

Robbie and Florida were in their positions, ready and anxious. There was a mission to accomplish now, and Jacy was here to solidify it. Me, with my dumb-ass blind faith, had no idea how special a woman she really was, one who would risk everything to be with me.

Three Days Straight

Chapter 20

I guessed the time to be about six-thirty. As we approached land, we could see fisherman preparing their boats for the day's chores. Robbie guided the boat alongside the dock like a veteran. Freddy and Hakeem grabbed the ropes and tied us down. Florida came down to me and asked, "Gee, if you don't mind, I'd like for Jacy to come with me to see my mom."

"I understand. Y'all go. Do what you have to do and take my prayers with you."

"Thanks, Gee, I appreciate you Bro. Jacy, I imagine you might be hungry by now?"

"Yes, a little."

"Gee, you guys know where the store is. I'll take Jacy there to grab something real quick. In fact, I'll get the old man to give us a ride to the hospital up the road."

"Go head, Man, do what you gotta do. We'll be alright."

The two of them walked to the end of the dock and crossed the road to the little store where we had previously eaten.

Hakeem alerted Freddy, "Here come your Burrito Brothers, Freddy," referring to the little old men who had unloaded the fish before.

"And they got that same cart. I can't believe it's still rolling."

Hakeem remarked, "Heck with the cart, man, I can't believe the guys are still rolling."

"At least we know the routine now, fellas. Come on, let's get this assembly line started," I replied. I hadn't eaten in almost twenty-four hours. "The sooner we get this fish

over to the store, the sooner we'll be feeding our faces."
Before long, we had fish flying everywhere. We made it
easy for the Burrito Brothers this time.

Mom's breakfast was delicious. Fish and eggs never tasted so good.
We had toast and the coffee was so strong, I had to ask for more milk
to put in it. I could see the beauty of this little port stop. It had a real
home feeling. Since this was our second time here, everybody felt
more comfortable. We hadn't ventured out any further than within
eyesight of the boat. Not knowing what our plans were restricted
us. I wished that we could explore the village, but that wasn't why
we were here. It was unfortunate that we didn't know what the plan
was but that's what life is all about, adventuring. Who could say
this little village wouldn't be just as fascinating as Jamaica. I got
an authentic Cuban cigar from the store and took a walk. Robbie
accompanied me, smoking his usual.

"So what's the scoop, Gee?"

"What's the scoop about what, Robbie? I'm wondering
too. We got a few days left on our original time allotment,
but right now I don't know what the plan is. If we hung
around here for the remaining time, I guess that would be
all right with me. How about you?"

"No, Gee, I'm talking about Jacy."

"Good question, Cuz. I don't know what's going to happen
with her. It definitely was not my plan to bring her back
to the U.S. I know darn well she can't fly back to Jamaica
with no proper papers. Man, I don't even know. I know
she needs to call home immediately to let her folks know
that she is all right, though. In fact, let me find a phone
and do that right now, because she and Florida have their
minds on other things."

"Yeah man, I was wondering what made them dash off
so quickly."

"They went to see about Florida's mother."

"I know that, but why was it so important that Jacy go,
too? And what did Florida say about her stowing away on
his boat?"

I didn't want to go through all the trouble of explaining, so I said, "Robbie, why you asking me all these questions? Man, I'm caught by surprise by all this, just like you."

Robbie took another hit of his joint and started coughing.

"Boy, that stuff gonna kill you and make you stupid," I said. We turned around and walked back to Mom and Pop's store to find a phone. Even though Mom didn't speak English, I knew enough Spanish to get her to help me.

"Hello, Mr. Weber, this is Gee."

"Yah, Mon. Everyting okay?"

"Yes, sir, everything is okay. Jacy is fine that's what I want to say first. I want to explain why she is not there. I'm making this call for her because she is attending to a sick lady. I had to leave unexpectedly last night because the owner of the boat that brought me to Jamaica had a dilemma. His mother was very sick and he felt it was important for him to be with her."

"Yah, Mon."

Jacy was very upset that I had to leave so quickly and hid onboard the boat. We took off and discovered her in the middle of the night. I knew something was wrong last night when she didn't answer the phone. I was worried knowing she was not at home but relieved when I saw that she was all right.

"Yah, Mon. Let me tell you something, Gee, dat you might not know,"

"Okay."

"When a woman love a mon, dere's noting dat she won't do. Believe me, dat's for sure. Me see her action every day, Mon. Compared to de oder boyfriend she have, you are very special. Me tink dat you are a good Mon and me want de best for me daughter."

"Okay."

"If dis what Jacy want, den it be okay wit me, you understand?

"Yes, sir, I understand."

"Me no worry, Gee. If Jacy wit you, me no worry."

"Thank you Mr. Weber. I don't know how long she will be assisting the lady, but I'll try to have her call you today."

"Yah, Mon, no problem."

All of us had been up basically all night long. Fishing and operating the boat gave us plenty to do. Dealing with the fish was real work. After Robbie and I came back from using the phone, we found Freddy and Hakeem on the boat knocked out. Robbie joined them. I would have too, but a full stomach, a rocking boat and me wasn't a good mix. Besides, the distant sky seemed dark out over the ocean and the waves were getting bigger. So for sure I wasn't going to subject myself to all that. A grassy spot on shore was waiting for me to stretch out on. From this vantage point, I could see Florida and Jacy approaching. A look of concern on his face was apparent long before he was within speaking distance.

"How's your mom doing, Bro?"

"She's in critical condition, Gee."

"Wow, man, I'm sorry."

"They got needles and tubes flowing in and out of everywhere. Mom had a heart attack right there on the dock. You know these are simple country people, they thought they could nurse her back to health. It took them a few hours to realize that she was sicker than they thought. The doctor says that the next few days will determine a lot."

"Well, we were going to spend a few days in Jamaica. I don't see any reason that we can't spend a few days in Cuba." I offered.

"I appreciate that, Gee. But to tell the truth, I don't know how long I might have to stay here. I was thinking that if you guys had to get back to the States, y'all could take my boat and I'll get back when I get back."

"Man, you crazy? How we gonna take your boat without you? Like we know how to operate that big ocean liner."

"Gee, you guys have been running the thing for the last couple of days. I've just been keeping an eye on everything."

"Well, like I said, the guys and me aren't that pressed, so as far as I'm concerned, we can lay low right here. Besides, I understand that Cuba is an interesting place anyway. I do have to get Jacy comfortable, though."

"Okay, Gee, how about me getting you two a room. Pop can give us a ride. Remember, we got a load of fish to barter with. Jacy probably wants to hit a place to buy whatever personal items she needs. We can go from there."

"Sounds like a plan to me. Is that okay with you, Jacy?"

"Yah, Mon."

"Where are the fellas, Gee?" Florida asked, looking toward the dock.

"They're knocked out on the boat. Let me take Jacy over to use the phone and we'll be ready to ride."

"Cool, that'll work," Florida replied.

As Jacy and I walked over to the store she spoke up.

"Me know dat you are upset for what me did, Gee. Me long for you so dat me couldn't bear to see you go so quickly. Me hope dat you forgive and not begrudge me."

"I phoned your Dad a little while ago and had a good conversation with him. I understand why you did what you did. Baby, somehow we gonna make the best out of this situation. How did your session go with Florida's mom?"

"She be fine when de cock crow 'tree day straight."

"Huh?" My expression showed my complete bewilderment.

"Me say dat she be fine when de cock crow 'tree day straight." Tell dis to no one, Gee. She get worse before she get better. Me have to see her again tomorrow at de same time. 'Tis very important dat me see her de same time each day."

"Don't you think you owe me an explanation about what it is that you do?"

"What you mean, Gee?"

"Oh no, don't act like you don't know what I'm talking about."

"Gee, do you tell me everyting dat you do?"

"What do you mean, Sweetheart?"

"Do you tell me where you are when me call at night and you not home?"

"Keep talking."

"Do you tell me how much money you got?"

"No, you don't need to know that."

"Okay den, Mon, you understand de point me make. Dere are some tings dat you don't need to know. But me trust you and have fait in you. Me want you to have trust and fait in me too. Remember dat. Me love you very much, Mr. Howell. 'Tis all you need to know."

Apparently, business was good for Mom and Pop at their restaurant/ store. I understood they owned the small hotel Pop took us to. There was family working at both places. The room wasn't anything but a simple, basic room in a cinderblock building. It had a small refrigerator and TV, no phone, no frills. Jacy pointed out the hospital where Florida's mom was as we headed to the room. There was a shopping area within walking distance, as was the boat, if you felt that energetic. Capo had just a two-lane highway going in and out. I helped Jacy determine what we wanted to do next. Since she had to get a change of clothes, it meant that we'd have to go exploring the shopping area.

"Hey Baby, you tired?"

"No, not too much. Me okay."

She was much younger than me and, of course, women like to shop, so I kinda had an idea what she wanted to do.

"Well, let's keep on pushing and see if we can get that pretty dress you been wanting."

"De pretty dress will have to wait, Mon, dere are more important tings me need right now."

"Right answer! You've just won the jackpot prize of a kiss from The Geeman!" I gave her a big smack on the cheek. We locked the door to our room and started walking toward the town area.

The sky had gotten darker over the last two hours, which held off the afternoon heat. Obviously, rain was coming; we just didn't know when. It took about two hours to find what we needed: personal items, three cute short sets, and enough underwear to last a few days. Since we had a refrigerator, we thought it would be a good idea to bring back some snacks for later on. We had been up all night and standing on our feet nearly two hours did us both in. Jacy couldn't get in the tiny shower fast enough.

"Gee, dey got no hot water."

"Good, you feel at home then, huh?" Jacy laughed. By the time I showered and came into the room, she was out like a light. Unfortunately, the room wasn't air-conditioned but the clouds held off the midday sun and there was a strong breeze coming through.

Sometime during the night, the sound of thunder woke me to close the windows. The wind had picked up quite a bit and the rain had started. Jacy and I were wide awake now with only a small lamp beside the bed to light the room. We fixed a snack and sat on the bed with nothing much to do but listen to the sound of the rain.

"I sure am glad we decided to get this room," I said.

"Yup."

"I wonder if the guys are still on the boat."

"Do you tink de rain be gone by de morning, Gee?"

"I hope so, Baby." We were out of touch with everything. We had no sense of time, no newspaper to read or radio to listen to. I thought it foolish to turn the TV on with all the lightning. "Hey Baby, give me some of your wine

146

flavored kisses." We played with each other and fell asleep again.

I awoke to Jacy shaking me. "Gee... Gee."

It took me a second to realize where I was. "Yeah Baby, what's up?"

"'Tis time."

"Huh?"

"Me have to go see Florida's mudda."

"Jacy, listen to the rain. Baby, it don't sound too good out there."

"But me have to go or de time spent yesterday be in vain."

"But how you going to get there? Where's Florida? Where's Pop?" Jacy put on the clothes we bought yesterday. "Where's anybody?" I looked out the window. "Baby, the sun hasn't even come up yet!"

"De rain almost stop, Gee. Me have to get to de hospital."

"Okay, Baby, if you're going I'm going with you." I don't think I had ever gotten dressed so quickly. To catch up with her I couldn't even think about brushing teeth. As I locked the door, I still hadn't put on my shirt. Jacy was thirty steps ahead of me and the hospital was half a mile away. Halfway there, we were already soaked. The eye of the storm had passed, but there was still a steady drizzle coming down.

"Gee, de clouds block any sunrise dat might be happening. De cocks no crow today."

I had no idea what time it was. But the cock not crowing made sense to me since there was no sunrise. I remember all the noise they made at Jacy's every morning. I just never realized they were quiet when there was no sunrise.

"Florida's mudda get better, but after de cock crow tree day straight. Me pray dat she hold on till den." I didn't realize Jacy could walk so fast. The importance of what she was doing was manifested in her drive to get to the hospital. She almost had me jogging. We raced up the gravel driveway, past a parked ambulance, and into the waiting area to see Florida stretched across three chairs. There were other people there, but he stuck out like a sore thumb because he was the only one so openly stretched out. Jacy shook him to wake him up.

"Florida... Florida! 'Tis time, wake up, Mon. 'Tis time."

"What time is it?" he sat up groggily.

"Me no know, but we must go to your mudda now." Without either of them saying another word they disappeared down the hall. I was wet and miserable. I felt for Jacy because she was just as wet as I was. I couldn't sit and it was cold. I had no idea of how long it was going to take them to do whatever they were going to do.

The attendant at the check-in desk was a very picturesque woman with exceptionally long blond hair. "Ma'am, I'm with the gentleman that was sleeping over there."

"You mean the guy that has been here all night?"

"Yes Ma'am. If he and the lady that was with him come back anytime soon, please tell them I went to get some dry clothes for the lady. I'll be right back."

"Sure, no problem."

"Thank you very much."

Since I was by myself, I jogged all the way back. The half-mile was easy. I changed clothes and got some for Jacy. Some of the family members who ran the hotel were moving around now. I asked for a ride and one of the fellas was nice enough to accommodate me. I gave him a couple of bucks and was back at the hospital in twenty minutes.

"Ma'am have my friends come out yet?" I asked the attendant.

"No, sir, not yet." They appeared in another five minutes. Jacy was shivering.

"Oh, tank you, Gee." I gave her the clothes and she immediately found the bathroom to change.

"How's she doing, Florida?" I inquired about his mother.

"Gee, this is about to beat me to death, Man. It just might be her time."

"Don't give up, Bro."

"I think the machines are keeping her here now. I don't know what to do, man." He walked away and sat with the people I suddenly realized had been on the boat with us. Jacy came out dressed in the dry clothes I'd brought.

"You feel better, Baby?"

"Much betta. Tank you, Gee. You are very toughtful." Florida came back to where we stood.

I think she saw the hopeless look on his face. She touched him and said, "Don't lose fait, Mon. Me come one more time tomorrow at de same time. Since you are family, you must be here to escort me in."

"Thank you for your help, Jacy." Florida replied, and solemnly returned to the waiting group.

Jacy whispered in my ear, "We must pray dat she hang on till de cock crow tree days straight. Do you understand?" I nodded. By now we had learned how to catch a taxi, so we headed back to the hotel. The drizzling rain had stopped and the sun was trying to peek through the clouds.

Earlier that day, we had left the room too quickly to brush teeth and do all the other things you ordinarily do in the morning. After we got back to the room, we got a chance to do all those things. Since we had learned where the shopping area was, we decided to go there for some breakfast. Capo Lucrecia was different than any place that I had ever visited. The structure of the buildings, the old American cars, and even the language was different, even though I knew enough Spanish to get by. In that sense, it was like Jamaica, because if the natives didn't want you to know what they were talking about, they knew what to do. After walking around and not really seeing anything that would interest a Jamaican or

American palate, Jacy suggested we go to the grocery store to take advantage of the wider variety. You can never go wrong with bread, meat, and cheese. We had drinks already, and I even bought a can of pork and beans. All I had to do now was find a way to open and heat them. As we approached the hotel, we saw the Three Stooges trying to fire up a barbecue grill.

"Yo, Fellas, I see you found shelter from that storm last night."

Freddy spoke first. "Man, that boat was tossing and turning and turning and tossing; and the sky was blacker than Ned the wino that hangs out by your house, Gee."

"Ah, ha. Ah ha." I faked a laugh.

"We had a meeting of the minds and figured it was time to un-ass that sucka," Freddy went on. "Pop at the store hooked us up. We couldn't tell him what we wanted. We looked like lost puppies, so he brought us into the fold."

"Hey, Jacy. You look refreshed today. How are you feeling?" Robbie asked.

"Fine, and you?"

"Good. You see we found this grill and hit the store, so we trying to get a little sump'n sump'n together." Robbie replied. "Did that storm scare you?"

"Yup, but me had Gee wit me, so me had protection."

"I was wondering where you guys might be." I interjected. "That daggone boat was the last place I wanted to be last night."

"Gee, that boat would've had you sick as a dog. It had me on the way by the time we decided to leave it," Hakeem admitted.

Jacy and I took our things to our room and came back out with whatever contributions went well with what the guys had. They said they found everything they needed at Mom and Pop's store. They had hamburger, barbecue sauce, and even some kind of Cuban beer. Each room had a sitting area outside. I brought a couple more chairs over.

Freddy cracked, "Look fellas, Gee can't get that furniture moving urge out of his system."

"I would've asked you to do it, Freddy, but I was afraid I was going to have to pay you," I snapped back.

"Yeah, you know anytime I pick anything up, I got to get paid," he replied

"Y'all know Florida's mom is not doing too well. Jacy and I paid a visit to the hospital this morning. Unless his mom has a drastic change in her condition, it doesn't look like he'll be leaving anytime soon. He doesn't know what he's gonna do. We've got to make some decisions; we can only stay here so long, you know."

"We left Atlanta last Sunday morning. Today is Thursday, and we planned to be back by Tuesday at the latest," Hakeem said, starting our deliberations.

"So it sounds like we have to leave here sometime Monday." Robbie added. Everybody was quiet as we continued preparing our food.

"All right now, don't everybody speak at once," Freddy declared. "Sounds like we got a per-dick-a-moment here. Let's tell the truth. We got a stowaway; a captain that don't know his way; and a boat a storm just tried to blow away. Sounds like we up Doo Doo Creek to me."

"Freddy, you know you stupid," I said, as we all laughed.

"Well, I'm just telling the truth. Y'all can spruce it up all you want, but that's the way I see the situation. Whose bright idea was this trip anyway?"

"Well as far as Jacy is concerned, she and I got that covered. If push comes to shove, Florida said we could take the boat back to Miami and not to worry about him. He knows how to find a way back."

Hakeem looked surprised. "Well I'll bait the hooks on the way back. I know how to do that."

Robbie interjected, "And I got the steering wheel."

"And who's supposed to navigate that big-ass ocean liner?" Freddy asked.

All eyes turned to him in unison. Even Jacy caught on and quickly pointed at Freddy. "Problems solved," I declared.

"Yeah right, y'all crazy if you think I'm going to get on a boat that Robbie's driving and you expect me to tell him where to go. All y'all done bumped y'all heads. Did y'all see all that vast enorminitity out there in that water?"

"Freddy, where you'd get that word?" I cracked. "See, you're smarter than you think when you wanna be. So, since all our problems are solved now, we might as well hang out here for the next couple days, make the best of things, and hey, are those burgers ready yet?"

"Yeah, Gee, the burgers are ready but all our problems have not been solved." Freddy remarked as if the weight of the world was on his shoulders.

"Freddy stop crying, I'm fixing my baby a beef barbecue burger. You want some chips too, Jacy?"

"Yup."

"Dat's my baby. Thank you Lord, hallelujah and amen. Now let's eat."

The Juke Joint

Chapter 21

The day progressed into evening. One of the family members, suggested that we visit a place with live music he thought would interest us. Pablo, who I understood to be Mom and Pop's nephew, owned the car in which I had ridden to the hospital that morning. A strikingly good looking man in his mid twenties, I wondered if he genuinely wanted us to be entertained, or if he just wanted to get in our wallets. Pablo's car was raggedy, but his driving skills were good and obviously it worked for what he needed. I conveyed our appreciation for his suggestion. The sun had gone down a couple of hours earlier and we needed some entertainment, so we accepted his invitation. Jacy was part of the gang now. We all piled into Pablo's car. How these old, worn-out, beat-up American cars still function over here, I'll never know. By every definition of the word, Pablo had a 'Plucka.' I couldn't be mad because it came through more than once. The fifteen-minute ride took us to a rural area on the outskirts Capo. We pulled up to a free-standing cinder block building that reminded me of a southern juke joint.

Pablo spoke no English, so I was the interpreter for the group. Recorded music spilled out the door and filled the gravel parking lot. A few folks milled around outside. Our colors of skin matched their different shades so we didn't stick out like sore thumbs. Had they spoken to any of us, it would've been obvious that we were visitors. Pablo said not to worry about anything because we were with him. We entered without a cover charge and found a table to accommodate the six of us. The waitress that came to help us had a smile a mile wide; a big healthy lady. This dear girl was the Cuban version of somebody's Big Momma, as nice as she could be. No one knew what to order. Pablo and I helped the guys order the beer they had bought earlier. It seems they thought it was adequate for something that was new to them. Jacy, not being a beer drinker, decided a mixed drink would be ok. In my broken Spanish, I asked the waitress to make a suggestion that was sweet with plenty of ice. I told her we weren't hard to please. Jacy and I shared. There may have been twenty-five people in the place. As time passed, the crowd, grew to fifty, then seventy-five, then standing room only. Pablo said this was the place to be if you wanted to hear good music, and that a band would be starting soon. The DJ stopped his music and announced "Los Hacedoros de Suenos." A conga player came out first by himself. It seemed like he was just warming up but as others joined one by one I could see the creative introduction unfolding. As each joined, the room lit up with more and more energy. A couple walked into the dancing area and was joined by others. I could see it coming - in a matter of minutes, this place would be off the chain. When the trumpet players finally took their places, the floor was full. Music was bouncing off the walls.

I thought, "Now this is some real music." I could see on the gang's faces that they were enjoying themselves. I gave Pablo the thumbs-up signal.

"Man, these guys are jamming," Freddy said as he pounded the table like he was one of the musicians. The introduction ended and the second song started with no further ado. The floor was full of picture-perfect salsa moving in sync with African-flavored drumming. An assortment of horns mixed in perfect harmony.

I couldn't contain myself, "Yeah!" I yelled. "Now dat's what I'm talk'n 'bout!"

"Oh yeah?" Jacy stood and pulled me to the floor.

I tried to shout above the happening atmosphere, "Baby, I can't do anything with this."

"Yes, you can, now come."

I threw up my hands like, "What have I got to lose?" We got to step'n and prep'n. I was trying to get-it-on. Jacy had me spin'n and grin'n and smiling ear to ear. The band was blasting and lasting and not about to stop. The place was lit to the max.

When we spun back by the table, I yelled, "Get out the fire

extinguisher! The place is on fire!" This was the Cuban version of what I had seen back in my Army days. I remember one of the best times in my life was in an Arkansas juke joint. This version was just as wild, only minus the jar of pickled pig's feet on the bar. Pablo couldn't have invited us to a better place. Before long, Jacy and I were drenched in sweat.

It was late by the time Jacy and I showered and settled in for the evening.

"Gee, 'tis very nice to be wit you away from home. Dat was fun dis evening. Me know dat when you left Atlanta, you hadn't imagined dat your trip was going to be anyting like dis."

"Yes, that's absolutely true. Jacy, as tough as some times have been in my life, I've learned to just roll with the punches. It could always be worse. You know I was complaining about my feet hurting one day until I saw a man that didn't have any feet. Do you understand what I mean when I say that?"

"In oder word, no matter how bad stuff get dey could always be worse."

"Yup, so I just try to be thankful for the blessings I have and keep on pushing. Look at my boy Florida having to deal with his mother right now. Who is more important to you than your mother? No one. I'm sure he would do anything to ensure that she gets better."

"Him just don't know dat in time, she get better. Dis me know, Gee."

"I already asked Pablo for a ride to the hospital in the morning."

"Oh, me don't mind walking, Gee."

"I don't either, but it's a little late and we don't want to oversleep.

"Yes, 'tis de last day for me to see her."

I awoke to see Jacy sitting on the edge of the bed. I had no idea how long she had been up.

"Good morning, Gee."

I hadn't moved a muscle, only opened my eyes. "Girl, you be tripping me out. How did you know I was awake?"

> "With me in you corner Gee, dere's noting you can't do.
> Me got your back. But right now, we have plenty of time
> to go before de sun come up."

The surprising things that had been revealed to me about Jacy convinced me to have faith in her. I appreciated the burden of wonder being lifted. Jacy once had sent a chill through my body by touching me. She told me about this trip before I did it. My conclusion was this: If I could have faith in God, whom I'd never seen, then I'd be foolish not to have faith in Jacy as a result of the things that I had seen. Jacy's extra eye, ear, and sensory perception gave me security. I didn't know what to call it, but I knew, if she said everything was going to be all right, then that was alright with me.

Diversions Need Prayers

G etting out of bed wasn't easy. We had stayed up late. Traveling and keeping odd schedules over the last few days kept me off balance, sometimes even wondering where I was waking up. After a brisk half-mile walk, I was wide awake. We looked around the waiting room when we arrived at the hospital, but Florida was nowhere in sight.

"Good Morning." Jacy addressed the blond headed nurse at the receptionist desk.

"Good morning to you too." She replied with have-a-wonderful-day attitude.

"Gee, me need for Florida to be here. Dey not going to let me see him mudda without him escort."

"We'll give him a few moments to get here, Baby. If he doesn't, then we'll have to think of something different. You're right though, Jacy, they're not going to let you see her without a family member present." I could see her nervousness. Her foot was tapping, and she kept staring at the emergency door through which we thought Florida would enter.

"Gee, Florida not coming, maybe him sleep too late. Him worn out dese last few days. Time is running out, me must go now before the sun come up."

"Okay Baby, I'm ahead of you. Check this out. I'm going out to that ambulance to see if the door is unlocked. If it is, I got a plan." It took thirty seconds for me to walk out to verify what I thought was true. If there were an emergency, I wouldn't think they'd want to fumble with keys trying to unlock doors. I could see the sun coming up over the horizon. "Yes, Baby, it's time," I whispered to Jacy when I came back. "Act like you have to go to the bathroom. When you hear a siren go off, I imagine the attendant at the desk will have to go outside to see what's happening. If you keep the door cracked, you can see when she leaves her desk."

"Gee, me scared."

"Scared, scared of what? Baby, time has run out and we don't have any more to play with. Hey, I got faith in you right?"

"Yes, Gee."

"Well, Baby, you got to have faith in me, okay?"

"Me do, Gee, but me so nervous dat me can't concentrate even if me can get to her room. Me waste dis most important session if me not settled and relaxed."

"Jacy, the sun will be up shortly. Come on now, we can do this. I'll meet you back at the room."

"Okay, Gee." Jacy got up holding her stomach like she had to go to the restroom. She walked quickly as if she needed to go immediately. The attendant acknowledged Jacy's presence with a nod. I watched the nurse waiting for the appropriate opportunity to disappear without drawing any attention. We had to act fast to prevent the sun's rising from catching us by surprise. Without hesitation, I opened the ambulance door and found the switch. The siren's decibels pierced my ears. The sound was deafening. I casually walked away and around the corner of the building trying not to draw attention on myself. My planned disruption covered the whole vicinity for quite a while. I thought it rather odd that no one turned it off in about thirty seconds or so. By that time, I was well away from the premises, appearing completely innocent of any wrongdoing. My part of the plan was finished. I wouldn't know if it was good enough for Jacy to get to Florida's mother and do whatever she had to do, until she was back at the room.

Now I was nervous. Not knowing drove me crazy and I had no way of easing my uncertainty. I turned on the TV, but the reception was lousy. We didn't have a stove or breakfast food so I couldn't start that. The dirty clothes were pilling up fast in the corner. I thought we'd have to find a way to laundry them today. A knock on the door gave me a bit of relief, thinking Jacy had made it back already. To my disappointment, it was Pablo asking if we were up and needed a ride. I told him no thank you and that we'd been there already. Guessing by the amount of time it had taken Jacy and Florida to see his mom the last time and for Jacy to walk back, I figured she needed an hour at the most.

A lot rested on this hunch that Jacy could bring relief to the sickly old lady. Florida wasn't going anywhere if his mother was dying. As a matter fact, I couldn't blame him. I wouldn't be thinking about anything else, either. Unfortunately, her condition determined what five other unrelated people were about to do. Florida was partly to blame. We didn't know he was making an illegal trip across the water, making us undocumented visitors. Obviously, she had been illegally living in the States the whole time, so I understood him bringing her back in the manor in which he did. Acquiring some of his father's habits, he didn't think he was doing anything wrong. It would've made no difference if Jacy's dream had included the part about his mother having a heart attack. At the time, to me it was just a dream, even though coincidental. My nervous pacing didn't help settle my mind. I recalled her also saying something about my head on her stomach and the weight disturbing her. If the dream was a forewarning, then it would be good to know why the weight part disturbed her. Jacy needed three days straight to see Florida's mom, and now three good sunrises for the roosters to crow. Today was the first; I had heard their noise on my way back. Truth reveals itself. Either Jacy's 'powers' are real or just cheap tricks that are quicker than the eye. In two more days, we would have to leave to go back to the U.S. with or without Florida. We'd see if he was sincere about our taking the boat without him. I thought, "This is another fine mess you got yourself into, Buckethead."

Two and a half hours had gone by, evidence that something was wrong. I didn't want to leave the room not knowing what was happening. I must have looked out the window a hundred times. My wet armpits made me change shirts again. Jacy's expected knock on the door frightened me.

    "Girl, where you been? What went wrong? Did everything

come out all right?" I realized I wasn't giving Jacy enough time to answer.

"Gee, relax. Florida was in de room wit him mudda sleep, Mon. When me come in he go out so me have peace and quiet. Me not nervous. Me have good session wit him mudda. She a good receiver, Mon. She lay quiet at peace. She a good receiver."

"I'm glad to hear that. Now I can relax a little."

"No, Gee, not yet. De policemen come and dey look for you. Dey tink you de Mon dat disturb de peace," Jacy replied with a bit of a giggle.

"Oh, that's funny to you that the police are looking for me?"

"Me no tell dem noting. Dey speak Spanish and me say me don't understand. Dey go get someone dat speak English but den me speak in patois!" She let out a full laugh now.

I had to chuckle myself, realizing that I'd have to lay low for the next couple of days and avoid the hospital. This was the last place I needed to go to jail, illegally visiting Cuba. Horror stories of people jailed in foreign countries just sprang into my head. "What took you so long getting back to the room?"

"Me go to de restaurant by de boat so dey no follow me to dis room. Gee, de lady dere make good fish breakfast. Me wait around for a while so me sure nobody follow."

"Well, I'm glad you're back and everything came out okay. All we have to do now is have you work your voodoo."

"Gee!" She shouted at the top of her lungs. She took a step back as her eyes fired up. "Never say dat. Don't you ever let me hear you say dat what me do be voodoo. Do you understand?

She'd caught me by surprise by how quickly and harshly she'd reacted to my insensitivity. "I'm-I'm sorry," is all I could stammer. I didn't realize the slip of the tongue would be so offensive. I tried to hug her, but she pulled away and walked outside. Since she didn't want to see me and I didn't want to see the police, I decided to stay in the room.

The police were familiar with Jacy's face, but not mine. Capo was such a small place, I figured it was a good idea for us not to be seen together publicly. Ideas kept creeping into my head about jails in places like this. We weren't even supposed to be here, and there was a U.S. ban on trade with Cuba. It was better for Jacy to hang out with the peanut gallery today. I upset her with my remarks, so that was another reason for us not to be together. Staying in the room all day was tough. It was hot, the TV wasn't very entertaining and I didn't even have anything to read. I was singing the blues. I hadn't eaten anything substantial all day, so decided to walk to the market area to find something. I didn't think the police would bother me. I could remain hidden among the people in the streets. As I walked past a place called 'Mi Cocina,' the aroma of something spicy made me turn around. Mi Cocina was just off the main street and had some tables out front. There was a table on the inside, but the cooking made it too hot to eat there. A canvas awning over the tables outside provided some escape from the afternoon sun. The restaurant had a home-style atmosphere and typical Cuban-flavored music playing in the air. The food was behind a glass display so you could pick and choose what you wanted. The broiled chicken marinating in its own juice caught my eye. I pointed to cabbage and peas, and I was in business. Other than myself, there was one couple eating on the picnic style table beside mine. I wasn't familiar with the flavor marinated in the chicken, but it was delicious. I was hungry, sure, but even if I wasn't, that food still would have been slam'n. Five minutes into my finger licking, salsa music enhanced delight, two uniformed walking cops turned the corner of the restaurant.

Panicking, I choked and almost peed on myself at the same time. They seemed to be arguing about something as they walked ten feet in front of my table. I regained my composure, but the urinating urge still remained like crazy. In the midst of their rapid-fire Spanish, I picked out the words "agua frio" for cold water. They turned and walked towards the aisle created by the two tables. I turned my head away. I held my breath and prayed the 'Please don't let them take me to jail today' prayer. As they kept talking back and forth they went in and asked for a drink of water. I didn't dare turn or look as they stood talking and drinking.

My concentration now was on restraining myself from peeing at this very second. As a grown man, I knew I couldn't sit right there and pee on myself. I had noticed previously that the small place didn't even have a restroom to wash my hands before ordering my food. I couldn't hold it any longer. I casually got up and walked into the small aisle created by the two closely situated buildings. My hands still greasy from chicken, I unzipped my pants just three steps into the pathway. I thought "damn... damn.. damn, now I'm going to jail for public indecency." As soon as my buddy found fresh air I pushed as hard as I could continuing my walk to the rear of the buildings over the ground on which I was peeing. Just in case the cops were behind me watching, I let my buddy go and held my arms down in the causal walking position, still praying the 'don't let me go to jail today prayer.' Unfortunately for me, my flaccid friend didn't have any control over the direction he was dismissing himself. The buildings were short, but I was pushing so hard and I didn't want to go to jail so bad that I finished not completely, but adequately enough to put my buddy away and keep on stepping as if nothing was the matter. If leaving half of that delicious, chicken dinner was the price I had to pay for not going to jail, then I just had to leave it. It sure was good, though.

When I got back to the room Jacy had hand-washed our clothes and was hanging them out back to dry. "If I hug you, will that make everything alright with you and me?"

"You don't have to hug me to make everyting okay. Why your pants wet in front? Me don't tink me want to hug you right now."

I looked down at my pants and said, "Oh... okay." I immediately went to the shower with my pants on. Of course I explained to Jacy what had happened. She laughed until tears fell. I thought the episode at the hospital that morning and the trip to El Cocina was enough excitement for one day. I decided we should have a quiet evening in the room. Jacy agreed.

My body clock woke me up at sunrise every morning. That had come to be my regular routine for years anyway, so it was nothing out of the ordinary. "I heard the roosters. That's good news, huh?"

"Yah, Mon, dat's good news. Me no need to go to de hospital today. Me tink one of de guys need to go to check wit Florida, dough. You should stay away."

"I'll ask one of them to go by and see how things are after a while.

Today was going to be a long day. We had to deal with a room with no air conditioning. Jacy and I weren't trying to be seen together in public. I couldn't speak for the rest of the gang, but I was ready to head back to the U.S. Miami was as close as a ten-hour boat ride. It was familiar ground. This was starting to be one of those occasions that make you appreciate there being no place like home. It was going to be different with my unexpected guest. I couldn't just leave her and if I tried to find her a ride back to Jamaica from here, she'd consider me a heartless SOB for the risk that she went through to be with me. I was tying to be positive and thinking that everything would work itself out. I had known Jacy for about four years. She was a good, honest, woman with "special powers," whatever that meant. Yup, if and when we made it back, life was going to be different. It was going to be a big surprise to some other people, as it was initially to me. That was another bridge to cross when I got there, but for right now, within about twenty-four hours we had to make some kind of decision. "Jacy I'm gonna head down to Mom and Pop's to get us some breakfast. Is that okay with you?"

"Dat would be okay, just take care and hurry back."

"Okay, Dear." I kissed her and headed out the door. I felt comfortable walking past the hospital. There were enough people on the road to disappear among. I was anxious to stop and see how Florida's mother was doing, but that had to wait. Her health was the determining factor in the safety and welfare of our trip home. As much as the guys had been operating the boat, I guessed we could make it back without Florida. If it were my boat, I wouldn't dream of letting anyone take it. Florida was responsible for us getting back, but obviously his need to be with his mother was more important right now. I could understand his rationale.

By the time I had gotten back with our breakfast, Robbie and Hakeem were sitting out front. Robbie was making his usual ritualistic contribution to his stupidity. Hakeem spoke up, "Yo, Gee, what's up?"

"Nut'n man, just chill'n. What's up witchu."

"Just chill'n, man."

"I hear ya. You straight?"

"Yup, I'm straight man. How bout you, you straight?"

"Yeah, man, I'm straight. Hey, check this out. You know we gotta get on up out of here by tomorrow."

"Yeah, I guess that is the plan."

"I kinda don't need to be seen at the hospital. Do you mind going by to see if you can run into Florida and ask him how things are going?"

"No, I don't mind. It's not like we got anything else to do. What did you do, wear your welcome out over there?"

"Yeah, something like that. You know we gotta head out of here tomorrow with or without Florida."

"What you got, some breakfast?"

"Yeah, I went down to Mom and Pop's."

"Well, I'm gonna head that way myself, I'll stop by the hospital on the way back."

"Jacy and I will be right here. We aren't going anywhere. Alright then, later Slater. "

"Later Slater."

Jacy and I killed the breakfast and were lying around enjoying each other's company for a couple of hours when someone knocked on the door. It startled me because I had just finished saying another 'Please don't take me to jail' prayer and the police were fresh on my mind. I had Jacy answer the door.

"Yo, man, how can you set up in here with the door closed as hot as it is?" Hakeem asked.

"We got this fan going, Bro, and that's about the best we can do right now. What's the lowdown?"

"His mom is still about the same and the police are looking for 'the man with the Jamaican girl.' What's that all about?"

"I had to create a way for Jacy to get in the hospital room yesterday and come to find out, Florida was in there sleeping. Had we known that he could have escorted her in."

"Huh? Something's funny, Gee."

"What's up, man?"

"Why was it so important that Jacy get in her room that you had to do something for the police to be looking for you?"

Jacy interrupted and helped him to the door. "Hakeem, you interrupting me time wit me Mon now, don't you have somewhere to go?"

"Well, excuse me, lovebirds," Hakeem said, as she closed the door behind him.

"Don't y'all be in there making any babies, either;" he called through the door.

Jacy replied, "Don't worry we will."

The afternoon heat was hard to deal with in the tiny room. The discomfort made us disregard our paranoia about the police enough to open the doors and let a breeze through. Between the TV, snacking, and each other, we managed to piddle around till the sun went down. Pablo asked if we might want to go to the juke joint again. We wanted to, but my fear of the police overrode the decision to go anywhere. Capo was a small place and I just didn't want to take the chance. Jacy could have gone with the guys but, still, her familiar face might prompt the police to interrogate whomever she might be with. I just didn't think it was worth the risk. They didn't feel too comfortable going out without me anyway because of the language barrier. We were all psychologically getting ready for whatever tomorrow would bring. The guys came and went throughout the day. One by one, they would stop by the room to talk. I could sense nervousness in all of them. Jacy was the most calm of the bunch. She was the one with an insight. She was the one who could tell me stuff before it happened. Why shouldn't she be calm? She displayed confidence in her abilities, which gave me more confidence in them as well. It appeared that Florida's mother would hang on until Jacy's prescribed time. That night, the moon shone clear in the sky. There was no forecast of a storm during the night. I wanted to hear some darn cocks crowing first thing in the morning. As crazy a wish as it was, that was what was on my mind. Jacy and I hadn't spoken about it all day, but she knew what I was thinking. Florida's mother had to show a significant improvement for him to feel comfortable about leaving her. I thought "Wow, what a lot to ask for."

Boredom having created the opportunity to play adult games all day, Jacy and I crashed much too early. We were wide-awake in the middle of the night, so naturally we found another game to play. By now, our body clocks were way out of sync, sleeping when we should be awake and awake when we should be asleep. We had no alarm clock to set or even a reason to set one. We were just there. Someone knocked on the door. Automatically, I jumped up too quickly to remember that I was not at home. The seconds it took to approach the door sobered me. I awoke Jacy; she pulled on a top and shorts to answer the door as I disappeared into the bathroom. I had to say my special prayer again.

> "Gee, it's Florida." The open door let in a ray of light that my eyes weren't ready for. The sun was up! The cocks had crowed! Florida entered the room grinning from ear to ear. He grabbed Jacy in a bear hug.

By his celebration, I knew what had happened. "Hey, man, you better let go of my woman! What's wrong witchu?"

> "Yesterday afternoon, they called in a priest to give my mom her last rites, she woke up this morning! By last evening, the doctor had given up hope, but she spoke to me this morning! They said we witnessed a miracle."

> "Stop!" Jacy commanded. We fell silent. She freed herself from Florida's grasp. She raised both hands in the quiet room, looked upward, and said, "De trut has come to pass. Jah make us not forget dat you send de sun and de rain and all blessings. Me tank you, Jah. Me tank

you for Florida and me tank you for him mudda." She stepped toward Florida slowly bringing her hands down on his head. "Go to your mudda now and say no more. We rejoice in your happy day but you speak of what has already come. Your mudda grow betta each day. Tell no one dat me be your intercessor. You must prepare now to return dese men to dere home."

Florida turned obediently and left. The room remained silent. I can't say that I was spellbound that Jacy's revelation came true, because this was another concrete example that she had a unique gift. A gift that had hinted of its existence twice before. This was more first-hand evidence. I had never spoken to the fellas about it. Florida didn't know he could expect his mom's improvement three consecutive sun-raised days after Jacy sat with her three days straight. I hadn't seen Florida's recuperated mother, but he wouldn't have been there if she hadn't undergone what the doctor called 'a miracle.' I've always known Jacy to be fair, honest, constructive. I had never known her to deal in foolishness. Her puzzle put itself together and I was the recipient of a blessing.

Two chicken Dinners To Go

Chapter 23

H unger and the afternoon heat led us to ask Pablo for a ride to Mom and Pop's. It was around lunchtime. The gang was there already. I paid Pablo, he said he'd be around back if we needed a ride. We pulled up chairs at their table as the guys continued eating. "How do you guys communicate and tell people what you want when I'm not around?" I asked.

Freddy stopped stuffing his face for a minute. "We don't have to say anything, Gee. Mom knows we like her fish. We just let her hook us up. In the morning it's with eggs, in the afternoon it's with salad, and in the evening it's with something that looks like potatoes."

"Hey, Jacy, how you doing?" Robbie asked.

"Fine and you?"

Robbie continued, "Yesterday, we thought we'd try some chicken. Freddy pointed at the ones running in the yard and flapped his arms. Moms got the idea. You ought to try it, Jacy."

Jacy replied, "Sounds like a good idea. Gee, what do you tink?"

"Huh?" My attention was riveted on a woman at a nearby table who was talking quietly on the phone.

"De chicken sound like a good idea," she said.

I called to Mom. "Senora, quiermos pojo por dos para llevar por favor."

"Hey, Gee, I don't appreciate you talking about me behind my back," Freddy remarked.

"I just ordered Jacy and me some chicken to go."

I directed Jacy's attention to the lady on the phone. "Baby, that's the receptionist lady who works at the hospital."

"Yup, wit long blond hair like dat Gee, she hard to miss."

When the woman noticed us looking at her, she turned her back to us.

"I think we got a problem, guys," I announced to the table.

"Yes, Gee, dere's a problem and it soon come," Jacy added.

"I hate to tell you this fellas, but lunch might be over."

Hakeem asked, "Yo, Gee, does this have anything to do with what we talked about yesterday?"

"Yeah, Bro, this is exactly what we talked about yesterday."

"All right so check this out, if that lady works at the hospital and something happened there that makes you stay away Gee, it looks like she's dropping a dime on you Cuz." Hakeem replied, after deciphering the situation.

"Yup. Florida came by our room a little while ago, fellas, and by what I understand, he's just about ready to go. I think I see a window of opportunity here."

Jacy interrupted. "When you see it open you have to move before it close."

"That's right, Baby. I'm gonna ease on around back like I'm gonna say hello to the chickens and persuade Pablo with a twenty-dollar bill, that you all have to go to the hotel immediately. He can drop Jacy off at the hospital on the way."

Freddy interrupted. "Excuse me, Gee, but does that mean that I have to leave this good meal Moms made for me?"

"Freddy shut up, this is not the time," Hakeem said tersely.

"I'll tell Pablo to keep the car running while you guys take

169

about eight seconds flat to get your stuff together. Here Hak, here's the key to our room. Robbie, you get Hak's stuff while he gets ours."

"Jacy, Florida has a lot of faith in you, Baby. If you tell him it's time to go, he'll listen."

"You guys don't let Pablo forget Florida and me on de way back," Jacy reminded them.

"I'll meet everyone at the boat as soon as possible."

"All right, Gee, you know you owe me half a lunch after this." Without answering Freddy, I casually stood up and walked to the rear of the building.

Pablo's eyes lit up when I handed him the twenty. He quickly rounded the building, started his plucka, and the gang was off. I figured it might take them ten minutes to go the short mile and come back. Hopefully, Florida was still at the hospital and would understand Jacy's urgency to leave now. There was no reason for him not to. By his account, his mother's recuperation was due to the 'lady with special powers' my friend, Robert back in Jamaica told him about.

Mom had our food together and insisted there was no charge. It was bagged up and ready to go. The hospital receptionist sat at her table attempting to eat nonchalantly, watching me watching her. There was no way to disguise my direct walk to the boat. Now it was a matter of who would show up first, the police or the plucka. I couldn't start the boat's engines. I didn't have the key. Had Florida gassed up? I was sitting on pins and needles waiting and wondering if I'd worn out my 'don't take me to jail prayer.' I just sat and waited, tapping my foot, not to salsa music, just nervous tapping. I heard car tires skid on the gravel road. When the dust settled, I could see the cops had won the race. The lone officer got out and answered a hand wave by the reporting patron still at her table. Pablo's plucka came in second on the ocean side of the road. Like a keystone cop movie, everybody exited the car at full sprint, luggage in hand like they were late to catch a flight. Florida was the first; he had nothing to carry. He dashed to the boat's helm and started the engines. By that time, I had unhooked the ropes tying us to the dock. Apparently, the policeman had been briefed but had to wait for an oncoming car to cross the road. He could see the race the group was running.

He found his break, crossed the road, and joined in. Policemen have a funny way of running. They have to hold their nightsticks and equipment from moving around. Luckily for us, this guy hung out at the tortilla stand more than the gym; he was kinda fat. The gang with its big head start won easily. Florida headed out to sea without even looking back. I gave the cop the bon voyage wave.

The Seasick Intrusion

Chapter 24

We left Capo Lucretia just after noon, so it would be somewhere around midnight when we got to Miami. To say the least, it was a relief to know we were finally heading home. Our captain was in place and we didn't have to worry about doing the trip ourselves. I was glad for Florida that his mother was doing better. He displayed such joy and appreciation to Jacy. His expression showed the weight of the world had been lifted off his shoulders. Everybody was feeling good. Jacy felt she'd done her job, and I didn't have to worry about cops. Everybody was relaxed, looking forward to being home.

Hakeem shouted from the lower deck, "Florida, are we going to do some fishing on the way back?"

"We might as well. You guys can have some to take back, and what you don't want, I know what to do with. We're going to have to stop and fuel up before long. Sorry, I have been kinda busy lately. It's no big deal; there are plenty of places we can stop."

We rode for a good two hours before we pulled into a dock. We all huddled around as Florida gassed up. I could see that it might be easy for someone to make an invisible trip to Cuba. There were all kinds of boats in the area and even more in the marinas. You could get lost in so much traffic.

Freddy remarked, "I'd hate to see the traffic jam if all these boats were at sea at the same time.

"Sometimes they are, Freddy," Florida replied as he finished refueling. "Holidays are the most busy, especially like Labor Day or Memorial Day. I try to not even go out on days like that." He headed back to the helm, but walked right back down. "My thermostat says that old Betsy is running a little hot, fellas. My mind was on my Mom back at Capo. I should have paid a little closer attention to the boat. "We're gonna have to give her a little while to cool down so I can check out the radiator."

I made up a quick song:
   "Well, y'all know
   that it's the time I go.
   I'm fine when it's moving
   but when it sits I don't be grooving."

That was my latest rendition of 'Lets Go for a Walk, Baby.'" I took Jacy by the hand and helped her off the boat.

"We'll sit for about an hour, Gee." Florida called out.

"Me see a store," Jacy yelled back.

"Uh oh, Gee, you in trouble now," Robbie replied. Everybody laughed.

Hakeem spoke up. "Wait a minute, y'all. I might as well come too. I might see something I want."

"Yo, Hak, bring back something cold to drink," Freddy yelled."

"I gotcha Freddy," Hakeen answered.

It was easy to mess around for an hour. The dock led to a main street shopping area. All this was new territory for us. We were exploring. We ducked into shops, trying to hide from the afternoon sun. Each place we entered had something different. One place was an ice cream shop. So, Jacy and I shared a cup of Cuban double-dip orange something. It sure was good. I let her have most of it. The treat was not something she would ordinarily have in Jamaica. I got a kick out of watching her enjoy it. Another place was a drug store that had Spanish language magazines. We giggled as we pretended to be able to read them just to steal some air conditioning. Hakeem made the last stop to buy beer. By the time we made a circle back to the boat, Florida had solved the problem.

"Yo, Freddy, better get one while they're cold," Hakeem called.

"Alright." Freddy grabbed one and chugged it down real quick. "It's hot and I was waiting for this. Which are two reasons for me to have another one. Jacy, would you like one?"

"Nope."

Freddy handed a beer to everybody else. "Do beer and ice cream mix?" I asked.

"Yeah, and when you finish that one have another," Freddy replied.

"No, thanks, one will be enough." Florida gave Robbie the thumbs up sign and he steered us back onto our pathway home.

It was a good day with no rain anywhere in sight. We were lucky, because we had left Capo so quickly, I don't think anyone had checking the forecast on their minds. Jacy and I still hadn't eaten the food from Mom's. There had been too much excitement when we first started out to think about eating. Mom's restaurant had spoiled me. Eating there had been quite a treat, ever since the first time we stopped there on the way down. Getting off the boat when we refueled allowed us to snack here and there. We had been riding again for a couple of hours and I figured in a while we would be nearing the halfway mark. Florida removed the cover of the engine compartment. He said that helped the engines run cooler.

Jacy asked, "Would you like me to fix someting to eat, Gee. Me get a bit hungry?"

"No thank you, dear, but you can have whatever you'd like. As a matter of fact, let me fix it for you." I went to the microwave and heated up a chicken dinner from Mom's. The aroma filled the kitchen cabin.

Hakeem got a whiff. "Watch out, Gee, I hear Freddy's stomach growling."

"Oh, he knows he owes me half a dinner still," Freddy said, glaring at me.

"Oh, I got your half a dinner right here." I replied as I discretely grabbed my crotch out of Jacy's eyesight.

Jacy sat down at the table and started to eat. I sat beside her, watching like a puppy waiting for scraps. "Me thought you said you no want none?"

"Oh, I don't want any, Dear."

"Den why you look like dat?"

"Like what? What are you talking about?"

"Here," she said pushing the full paper plate between the two of us.

"I didn't think it was going to smell this good, Baby." I ended up eating half.

The hottest part of the day had passed. The sun would soon sink over the horizon, making this the best part of the day to travel. We had caught a few fish, as the lines had been out for the last couple of hours. A change of music every now and then broke the monotony of the constant sound of the engine and waves. Occasionally, we saw other boats in the area, one of which looked like something from another era with huge white sails. Florida kept us informed with the details he knew about each. Jacy and I had an advantage because we had each other to talk to. We had a chance to talk about what was going to be once we got back, what to expect.

"Me finally get de chance to see how you live, Gee."

"Yeah, I'm looking forward to having you around."

Jacy had proved that there was no one like her. The gifts she had put her in a league all her own. Some people would call it voodoo. I didn't know what to call it. I wasn't afraid. By nature, people are afraid of the unknown. It definitely was new to me to actually see her talents implemented. But I wasn't afraid. I trusted that whatever 'powers' she possessed would be used with good intentions. She never talked of crazy, off-the-wall stuff. In fact, she never talked about her insights at all. I hadn't seen her head turn all the way around like in the movies, so I wasn't afraid. My baby was special, and that couldn't be anything but a contribution. Life was going to be different.

With Robbie and Florida taking turns at the helm, Florida would occasionally come down to the engine compartment and check things out. Obviously he was still concerned about the temperature of the engine. Knowing enough about engines, I knew that they sometimes ran hot. Overheating could completely ruin an engine. To prevent this from happening, you had to shut them down to cool off. It happened to my trucks every now and then. Hovering over the engine, Florida called up to Robbie, "What does the temperature gauge show now?"

"It's getting in the red," Robbie called back.

If my truck temperatures were running in the area marked in red, I would pull over immediately.

"Okay, Robbie, shut'm down," Florida called. The boat slowed and we stopped moving forward. Florida lowered an anchor and said, "we're going to have to sit for a while until the engines cool down, fellas. I'm sorry for the inconvenience. But while we're out here if y'all want to catch some red snapper, we can drop some lines down to the bottom where they are.

Thinking we might be here floating around for a while, I made a beeline to my medicine bag. I popped a pill, stuck a patch behind my ear, and hoped they'd get in my system fast enough for me not to get sick.

Freddy, being a pretty good mechanic, examined the engine with Florida. "You might have a leak in your radiator, but you have to wait for the temperature to cool down to take the lid off to see. If that's the case after it cools down, you can back the cap off a half revolution to keep the pressure from building back up again."

We pulled in the trolling lines that we used while moving and got the poles with lines that went straight to the bottom. We waited for the engine to cool and fish to bite. The boat bobbed in the Caribbean. Ten more minutes of bobbing went by. I jokingly whispered to Jacy, "Can you make the boat stop bouncing?"

"Only Jah can do dat."

Everybody was looking at me looking at them. I felt it coming as the boat continued to bounce and bob. I tried to make a joke to give everybody a hint of what I was feeling, "Jacy why did you make me eat half of your dinner? You know I wasn't hungry."

"Oh don't blame dat on me, Gee. Do you feel okay?"

"Nope."

"Think you're getting sick, Gee?" Florida asked.

"Yup."

Five more minutes of doing the Caribbean bounce and my head went over the side. Two more minutes had me barfing up everything I had just eaten. "Uuuuggghhhhh!!!!!."

"Now dat's what I'm talking 'bout," I heard someone from the peanut gallery exclaim.

The bad thing about barfing is that you never know when it's going to end. It's like when a good heave comes, you hope it's the last. I stood leaning against the side hoping that I was done.

"Uuuggghhhhh!!!!"

"Uh, oh, there goes round two." Unfortunately there was nothing anyone could do to relieve me. I hoped, out of the sympathy of their hearts, they would if they could.

"Uuuuggghhhhh!!!!" I got a quick reprieve long enough to moan, "Alright, y'all heathens can laugh later, but right now I feel like dog doodoo."

"Hey, Gee, that's Robbie and Hakeem cracking on you," Freddy sympathized. "I'm not laughing."

I got myself together and made a beeline down to the bathroom. "Uh oh I think it wants to come out the other end now," I recognized Freddy's voice.

There is no more terrible feeling than barfing. Needless to say, I hate doing it. It seems I almost pass out. Sometimes I wonder if other people heave and ho as intensely as I do. It seems my whole insides are being forced up. I sat in the bathroom for who knows how long as everything took its natural course. I prayed the 'Please make me feel better, Lord' prayer giving it a few minutes to reach him. For some reason, it never did. I didn't know what was happening with the crew. I was just trying to exist a few more minutes. Eventually Jacy came down and asked through the door if I was all right. I tried to make a moaning noise just to let her know I was still alive.

"Open de door, Gee," she demanded.

"Go away."

"Come now, Mon, open de door."

"I'm gonna die, right here on this toilet." I managed to pull my pants up. If I remember correctly, I washed my hands and rinsed my mouth out... I think. "If I don't make it tell the guys to throw my body over the side."

"Come lay down, Mon. You been in dere twenty minutes. Me tink you got no more to heave." Jacy helped me over to the bed. We sat there momentarily and removed our shoes preparing to lie down. I wanted the boat or the ocean to stop moving; either one wouldn't make any difference to me. I closed my eyes and could do nothing else but wait; wait for either the engine to cool or the boat to stop moving. The next best thing happened: I fell asleep.

The roar of an unfamiliar engine woke me. As I slowly came to my senses, I realized I was in a fetal position with my head resting on Jacy's bosom. She stroked my head like that of a baby, soothingly, as only a mother knew how to do. I weakly raised my head and looked in her attentive eyes. "Thank goodness I'm still alive."

"Just relax, Baby, we'll be moving before long."

Loud, commanding voices filled the air outside. I opened my eyes. Gruff unfamiliar language continued to break the routine sounds of the sea. I rose from the soothing warmth of Jacy's embrace. I saw a look of wonder on her face. My thoughts of "who... what" jumbled my reasoning. The sound of the turbo engine stopped followed by a jolting bump that reminded me of another automobile's bumper slamming into mine at a stoplight. Jacy and I stared at each other in utter confusion. Men started yelling, followed by the sound of rapid gunfire, sending panic through Jacy's body into mine. The air was charged with emergency. Panic had boarded the boat. We heard a second burst of gunfire mixed with more shouting and numerous thuds on the deck of the boat. Spent gun shells clinked as they landed. The commands were decipherable now.

"Get down! Get down now!" The smell of gun power overrode the cabin's sea scent. "No move!" An agony tempered groan followed a thud and more commands. "No move!" The island-accented voice commanded. Jacy and I sprang apart from each other; she fell into her original hiding position as I looked around for a spot to disappear. My aching chest and weakened body couldn't move as quickly as Jacy's. I needed healing time that I didn't have. I fell back into the fetal position minus my comforter.

We were floating helplessly somewhere between the straits of Florida and the island of Cuba. I drew the conclusion that we were being robbed, sea jacked. Out in the middle of nowhere, without Smith or Wesson within grasp. I cursed the clown's idea for this trip now. I couldn't run even if I had somewhere to run to. I listened to the sounds of the sea, heavy footsteps, the fish hull door slamming shut, and other compartment doors being opened and closed. These were the undeniable sounds of a thief. I knew it was just a matter of time before the bedroom door would open. Unbalanced equilibrium and now fear of the unknown froze my body. The plodding of the intruder's footsteps entered the living area. There were more sounds of compartments opening and closing. No one spoke. The air reeked of violation. Seconds of suspended unknown finally came to an end as the intruder's boot released the lightweight door from it's hinges. The door bounced off me to reveal a gun barrel pointed in my direction. "No move!" he commanded and stood there inspecting the room. I stretched out face down to show my empty hands, legs hanging half off the bed. He entered the room and delivered the full weight of his booted foot directly on my lower leg. That explained the previous moans of agony.

"Oh you son-of-a!!!!!!"

The pirate demanded, "No move!" as his gun in my face, cut short my explicative. He patted me down and found my wallet. Holding his gun, he removed the money and tossed the wallet to the floor. Jacy's hiding spot was immediately discovered.

"Come!" he ordered. I could see him help expedite her movement by grabbing her arm. She stumbled over the broken door and landed on the bed. "No move!" he commanded again. He checked the pockets of her shorts, found nothing, and slowly allowed his hand to roam the curves of her body. She forcefully flung his hand away only to have it's backside recoil squarely against her cheek. The sound of the assault landing on her face bounced off the walls. The impact sent her body rolling toward mine. Immediately, his gun touched my forehead to ward off any reaction that I may have had to his actions.

"You'll die before dis day be gone," Jacy declared, seething with anger. "Jah know it, and now you do too."

He raised his hand again to further warn her. "Shut up!" He spat and turned, continuing to go through any door or drawer of anything that appeared to be a compartment. I wanted this savage to find whatever he was looking for and leave. Thoughts of killing us, disabling the boat, and messing with Jacy flew through my head. With terror seizing the boat, it was impossible to determine how much time had elapsed. The intruder seemed to be in no hurry. Floating out here in the middle of nowhere presented no need for urgency. It was still daylight. They could see any impending rescue attempt long before it occurred. They left no space untouched. If the butt of his weapon wouldn't open a potential hiding place, his boot did.

Holding the weapon against my head, he ordered Jacy and me outside with the rest of the group. My body moved like that of an old man. He helped me along with his boot. I fell awkwardly against the wall on the deck and placed my hands behind my neck. In a half-sitting position, I could see everything. Everyone lay frozen in different positions. Jacy sat as close to me as possible. Hakeem's hand covered his head as blood trickled between his fingers. A small crimson puddle formed as the blood ran the length of his arm and dripped from his elbow.

The seriousness of our situation slowly dawned on me. The compartment that held our bags had been discovered. It looked like anything of interest was in a pile on the deck. In the brief second before I fell to the deck, I'd seen a speedboat closely connected to the side of ours. Now I could see another man with an assault rifle standing, watch over everything. If there were just two guys, how could we get them? What could we do? Even though my body was not at one-hundred percent, my mind was searching for a window of opportunity. We couldn't just let them kill us without putting up some kind of resistance. Their guns gave them total advantage.

They could kill any of us, at any time and sink the boat. I could see that Hakeem's pockets had been turned inside out. The intruder tossed his weapon to the man standing guard. He held both weapons displaying double power. The toothless snarl on his face expressly cast the aura that he smelled as bad as he looked. The intruder stood in the middle of his collected pile and went through Jacy's things first. He found nothing of interest, so he tossed them to the side. My bag was next and he proceeded to do the same with my clothes.

The next bag emptied made a thud on the deck. He picked out a block of something and said, "Ah ha, marijuana, amigo!" he exclaimed with glee in Spanish like he had just won a prize. He moved it over to what I presumed was his keeper pile. The next bag revealed two more blocks as did the last bag. He had already gone through the refrigerator and now was placing everything of interest back into the empty bags. It appeared as though our ordeal could be coming to an end. The best scenario would be for them to take what they wanted and just leave. That's what I was hoping for. The pain of his boot would subside; at least we had our lives. Hakeem was going to need some attention and soon, but at least he was moving. The watch guard laid down his weapons as the intruder tossed him their new possessions, leaving them temporarily vulnerable. If there was going to be an opportunity to save ourselves, it would be in these few seconds. My thoughts were, what if they kill us and I didn't do anything to try to save us. Any rescue attempt was going to take Robbie, Florida, and I right now, at this exact moment. Any flash of hope had to be coordinated, like the slip from the cops at Capo. But getting their attention right now was impossible. Besides, how could we leap the distance from boat to boat in that same instant?

This wasn't a James Bond movie. We were completely at their mercy. After they finished tossing their bounty, the intruder stepped across to join his comrade. The window just closed. I felt our narrow brush with death had come to an end. As long as we had been there waiting, barfing, dozing, and being robbed, the engine surely had to be cooled enough to start by now. The bandits stood face to face momentarily, conversing in low tones, hovering in venom. The overseer had already returned his weapon to its lethal aiming position. As a result of their conversation, the intruder reboarded our boat and pointed his weapon directly at each of us one at a time, allowing it to linger between each potential target. He then pointed it in the air and burst off another round of fire. The shells clinked on the deck again and a new wave of fear grasped us. I hinged on regurgitating again, this time from the sadistic scowl that floated from his being. The savage pulled Jacy to her feet and in the direction of their boat, he ruthlessly guaranteed death to anyone daring to stop him. The overseer fired his weapon also. Jacy, shoeless, left our boat without putting up a fight.

Jacy seated herself at the rear of their boat. The overseer took the helm as the intruder stood on guard with his weapon pointed at us. He remained there for perhaps the next fifteen seconds, which seemed like an eternity. We all stood dazed and confused for another fifteen as they sped away.

> "Robbie, start the engine." Florida ordered as he finalized the requirements for the engine. Freddy immediately assisted a groaning Hakeem. I couldn't take my eyes off the fleeing boat. The speed racer quickly put distance between our two boats.
>
> "Follow'em, Robbie!" Florida commanded.

Before Robbie could turn in their direction, I could see the intruder bending over the tossed pile. He stood back up and disappeared to an area under the helm. Jacy bent over also as if she was attending to something on the floor. For maybe ten seconds she was out of my sight as the speeding boat put more space between us. I didn't dare turn away for fear of never seeing Jacy again.

"Give it full throttle," Florida shouted. The front rose in the air as I changed my position to keep them in view. As swift as their boat was, there was no way we were going to catch them. There was nothing we could do if we did. As far as I knew, Florida didn't have any weapons. The sound of our engine compounded by the waves hitting the sides didn't silence the racer's turbo. It was now at a fever pitch, running at maximum. Maybe thirty seconds had passed since the thieves left. Jacy reappeared as she sat back up. She crawled to the top rear area behind the engine and either jumped or fell into the sea.

"She's in the water!" I yelled.

"I see," Florida answered, taking over the controls. "Keep your eyes on her!"

The racer immediately took the hardest turn it could possibly make to the right. It kept that position, making a complete circle back in our direction. Its front end rose up as it reached full speed from the torque of its engine. Florida maintained our forward direction, and still I didn't dare take my attention off Jacy.

"He's circling back around toward us!" Robbie yelled.

"No he's not," Florida replied. "There's something wrong with his boat! His throttle is stuck!"

We were getting closer and closer to the place where Jacy had entered the water. I could see her occasionally as my eyes searched the cresting waves. We were inside a huge circle the racer was making, still going at full speed. I felt the big fishing boat couldn't go fast enough in Jacy's direction. The pitch of the engines said that it was trying its best.

"Freddy, get a life preserver!" Florida ordered. Hakeem sat still on the floor holding a piece of clothing to his bleeding head. We shouted to be heard above the sound of the two boats' engines and the waves crashing against our sides. We were close enough to Jacy now, that Florida had to reduce our speed. I could see her clearly now as she floated on her back. She threw her hand up to either signal that she was all right or for our attention. The sound of the turbo engine got stronger as it made another circle closer to our rear. Robbie had come down off the top deck and started pulling off clothes. He was the first to hit the water. Adrenaline relieved my pain of being kicked and the agony of seasickness. Freddy followed my dive with a perfectly tossed preserver. Robbie reached Jacy first as I towed over the preserver. She gagged and choked on the salt water. The thought of sharks passed through my mind. The thought of never seeing my daughter again did too.

"Hang on, Jacy, we got you!" Robbie yelled, fighting the waves that soared around us.

183

I didn't realize how hard it was to battle them. I made it to Jacy with the preserver, a stroke after Robbie. The bandits' boat now was completely out of control and making an even tighter circle. It was obvious there was not going to be enough room in the circle, for both boats.

"Here, grab hold, Jacy!" I shouted. The sound of the turbo was deafening. As Freddy reeled in his human catch, I could see Hakeem holding a towel to his head. He hooked the aluminum ladder over the side with his free hand. Jacy was cognizant enough to help herself up the ladder, using all her strength.

"Come on, baby, you can do it." I coaxed her every step up the ladder. "Pull Baby! Pull as hard as you can." Freddy grabbed whatever clothing fit his hand and hauled Jacy over the side as we did the Amberjack with our fishhooks. I was next, and Robbie followed me out of the water.

"Go! Go! Go!" Freddy yelled to Florida above the turbo noise. We lurched forward into full speed as the three of us collapsed on the floor, Jacy from exhaustion. She gagged and spat as she kneeled on the deck. I kneeled beside her with my arm over her shoulder.

"It's okay, Baby, get it all out." We throttled further away, out of the tighter circles the out-of-control racer was making. Fifteen seconds at full speed elapsed with Florida at the helm. As more seconds passed, the more relief came over us. Thirty seconds more into our continued trip home, it was obvious the racer wasn't going to exit the pirouette in which it was stuck.

"Ah, man!" We exclaimed in unison, mouths gaping.

"Damn!" Freddy exclaimed. In the distance, we saw the boat's bow spiraling straight up. The boat seemed to screw itself into the ocean. We watched till there was no more to see as the huge waves took back their territory.

Dat's My Baby

The sun had gone down and complete darkness would soon surround us. Florida pulled out his first-aid kit. He dressed Hakeem's aching head and the bleeding eventually stopped. I felt the after effects of my seasickness, but now that we were moving again, I was going to be okay. It was my turn to soothe Jacy. She took over for me in the barfing department. Hers consisted of salt water and, thank goodness, only lasted a moment. I salvaged some dry clothes from the jumbled mess the thieves had made. When she got herself together, she went below to change. "You gonna make it, Baby?"

"Gee, dat salt water tastes so terrible when it go down. Me tought me gonna choke to death, mon."

"I saw you when you jumped off. I didn't take my eyes off you, Baby. Heading in your direction I was just hoping and praying that you'd hold on just a little bit longer. You were smart to float on your back like you did."

"Yup, me can do dat one all day long, Gee."

"Well, you did it good, girl. I'm so proud of you. You did a lot of things good."

"Me get it from you, Gee."

"I didn't do anything. Baby, you're the one that sent that boat out of control."

"You da one dat taught me about da window of opportunity. Me see it, and me take it."

All I could say was, "Dat's my baby!" as I held her like a prize, and rocked any discomfort away.

I knew that Jacy had special talents; I had seen them work more than once. I assumed that she called upon them to bring an end to this ordeal. I knew not to ask her about how she did whatever she did. Florida hadn't been a witness to any other manifestations of her talents. He had only known of her through whatever my boat-operating friend Robert told him. People are skeptical until we see verification with our own eyes. Florida's mom being so sick put him in a situation desperate to believe that Jacy could contribute to her recovery. Florida wasn't familiar enough with Jacy to know that she could have very well used her talents to put an end to our dangerous situation. The others weren't aware of anything. I figured someone would eventually ask her what she had done. We joined the others at the dining table.

We all needed to calm down. Robbie was doing the steering. "Man, my head is killing me." Hakeem moaned.

> "Hang in there, Bro. Here take a couple of these." Florida pulled some aspirin out of his kit. "I'll get you some water."

> "I remember lying on the deck, and then the next thing I remember is seeing you guys jump in the water. What happened in between?" Hakeem asked.

I volunteered, "Don't worry about it now Hakeem. Just be thankful we're all still here. We'll talk about it later."

Florida brought back some water for Hak to wash the pills down. He sat back down as Freddy asked," Jacy, I'm trip'n trying to figure out what the heck happened on that boat?"

I changed the conversation for fear of exposing her talents. "I'm just trying to figure out why there was marijuana on this boat."

Florida replied. "Me too, Gee."

> "I guess we can talk about that later, huh fellas, when Robbie can be around." I directed my comment to Freddy and Hakeem.

Freddy wouldn't say anything and Hakeem needed to recuperate.

Florida put on some oldies but goodies. Al Green was singing about love and happiness. At this point, we had nothing to eat and nothing to drink, which was not really a problem. With the interruptions of an overheating engine and thieving pirates, we had about six to eight more hours of traveling to do. We could make it that long without food. No one was interested in fishing. We were all still in various states of shock, that left us with nothing much to do. It was nice that we at least had music to listen to.

"Yo, Robbie, you want me to take over for a while?"
Florida called up to the helm.

"No man, I'm all right. You might want to come and check to see if I'm still on course," he replied.

I whispered in Jacy's ear, "Robbie doesn't want to come down here because he knows either Florida or I am gonna say something about what was found in their bags."

"Hey, I told y'all it was rude to whisper," Freddy remarked. I got the feeling he was trying to humor himself back into my good graces.

"Oh, you want to know what I was whispering about? Okay then, I said I'll bet Robbie doesn't want to come down here because he knows I'm gonna say something about what was in your bags. You know what, Freddy? I had absolutely no idea you guys would go out like that." I smacked my head with my hand and made a smacking noise with my mouth. "Boy, am I naive."

"Gee, Nobody would have known anything if we hadn't gotten jacked."

"Well, check this out, Freddy. What if those pirates had been the Border Patrol or immigration authorities? So don't even try to play like it was all right to try some dumb junk like that. Hey, but who cares? They take Black folks to jail everyday for messing with drugs. They don't care, they got plenty of room. They're building more jails all the time. I'm just tripping 'cause you three clowns' selfishness put this man's livelihood and other people in jeopardy. Now that sucks Freddy. That sucks and I'm done with it. It just lets me know where 'my boys' are coming from. I'm so hot I could spit, now that's what I was whispering about."

Jacy could see that the more I spoke, the more I excited myself. "Come, Gee." She pulled me by my arm back to the bedroom downstairs. I got up and was reminded that my leg was hurting. I stood there a few seconds to deal with the pain. Jacy helped me hobble away.

"De bandit put holes in de walls, Gee. Dey knew where to look." She said as we laid down on the bed.

"Baby, I can't believe those guys would do something so risky. I'm sorry."

"You don't have to apologize to me Gee, you didn't know I was going to be in de middle of all dis."

"I imagine those pirates would have been better off had you not been here. It shows they didn't know who they were messing with, huh?" I chuckled.

"You remember de first time you meet me at de cambio?"

"Yeah."

"Me don't say nut'n to you den cause me no know you dat well. But me get a bad feeling from yo friends when you shine like de sun. Every woman want to have a Mon, Gee. Dat's why me choose you. Jah tell us dat de trut come to light."

"What do you mean by that, Baby?"

"De trut come to light. Me get a bad feeling from dem and look what dey try to do. Dey don't care about you. Dey jus want what dey want. And look at you. Me get a good feeling from day one. You knew noting about dem plans. De trut come to light. Gee, remember de dream me tell you about before you leave?"

"Yeah, it was about our boat trip."

"And me confused about de weight of someting?"

"Yeah, I remember."

"It was de weight of what your friends were carrying. Me

188

put it together now. You understand?"

"Baby, I appreciate you more and more every day. I don't know what I did to deserve you." Saying that brought a smile to her face, which brought a smile to mine.

This trip was one of those that took me all the way out to the edge; like standing on the cliffs at Rick's in Negril, getting ready to dive. Getting a thrill is okay, but if I'd had a hint this would have turned out this way, it's one I could have done without. It would have been nice had Jacy's dream included all the details. Her stroking my head pacified me as I lay on her stomach. She brought me back to the realm of peacefulness. It was good to listen to the music and be in her calm serenity but I had had enough of the boat, the barfing, the bucketheads, and especially enough of the bandits. I was more than ready to be back at my house, in my own bed. Whoever came up with the phrase, "there's no place like home," knew exactly what they were talking about. We dozed off and woke up three hours closer to that place.

The group as a whole came limping home. The boat needed attention; Hakeem, Jacy, and I had been through our physical challenges; and if that weren't enough, trust in my gang had been destroyed. I had none, and I think Florida felt the same. What an ordeal; we were coming home like a lost dog with its tongue hanging out. Another hour passed and we got closer. Hakeem needed to go to the hospital for stitches, if nothing else. It appeared he'd have a headache for a while. We were beat and it was obvious. I figured we could pile in over at my cousin Quinn's, especially since we had no money for hotel rooms. It would be tough to drive all the way to Atlanta, even if Hakeem didn't need medical attention. We'd have to explain something to her. With our needing money and Jacy being with us, Quinn would expect some kind of explanation. Another hour passed, which meant that we were only another one away. We'd see lights before long. We'd be back in our own territory again, where we could be comfortable.

I get a secure feeling in the midst of familiarity. It would be new to Jacy, but even she would be under my wings' protection. She'd be in good hands. Besides, this is what she wanted. She'd been bugging me for the last couple of years to step up to the plate. After seeing what she showed me, I would be the benefactor of all she had to offer. Faint lights twinkled in the distance. Freddy was taking his turn at the helm, and Marvin was singing to his distant lover. Sitting at the eating table again, Florida spoke up.

"Jacy, I'm sorry this was not a pleasant experience for you. Believe me when I say that what happened is something that I've heard about but have never seen, and I've been boating all my life."

"Jah watch out for babes and fools. Me be eder one as long as he continue to watch out for me."

"My Father was a boater. I learned of some things he would do in the old days. I can't say that I was happy about some of those things. I imagine he did do some things that were improper, and I have too. But I always figured that for me life would be easier not having to look over my shoulder all the time. I'm trying to tell you, I owe you tremendously for the blessings you bestowed on my Mother."

"Me see yo heart, Florida, you deserve blessings. Jah know we are all human and make mistakes. Me throw no first stone eder."

"Thank you Jacy. I want you and Gee to know that if there's anything I can do to repay you, I'll gladly do without hesitation." The lights on the shore began to take on the shapes of buildings. We were getting closer.

"To say the least, Florida, this has been quite an experience." I sighed in relief.

"To satisfy my curiosity, am I allowed to ask what you did on that other boat to get free?" Florida asked Jacy.

Jacy looked at me and smiled. "Yeah, Mon, you can ask. Me tink everybody wonder."

"I've been trying to understand why that boat did what it did. I'd seen throttles stick before but I'm still wondering."

Florida and I sat on the edge of the kitchen chairs like children listening to bedtime stories, waiting for her explanation.

"Me know me had to do someting. Me see dat one Mon

drive de boats while de oder caught up in him new prize of what him take. When him take it underneat, dey leave me alone. You understand? De leave de top off de engine like yours and de toolbox sit right dere beside. Me see a window of opportunity and me work fast. Me see tin snips and start cutting as much as me can. When me tink me do enough damage me jab it in de top and jump off de boat."

"Dat's what I'm talk'n bout!" I exclaimed. "My Baby's tough, she don't play, Homeboy! Yeah!" We all started high-five'n, slap'n and dap'n. Our rejoicing ended in a well-deserved laugh. Robbie called down from the helm to see what all the excitement was about.

"Yo, what's up?" he asked.

Florida replied, "Nut'n, man, we just chill'n." Smiling at Jacy and I, he returned to take his place at the helm.

My closest guess would be that it was about four o'clock in the morning when Florida steered his big rig into its dock space. I was never so glad to get off the thing and set foot back on home turf. Watching Jacy, I expected a look of surprise or elation on her face as she stepped into her new beginning. She was as cool as if this was just another day. Our first priority was to get Hakeem some medical attention.

"Yo, fellas, in my card file at home, I keep a list of some of my regular customers. I got a doctor friend whose office is not too far. I'll be right back." Florida sprinted off.

When he got back, he took Hakeem to see his friend. Freddy and Robbie camped out on the boat, but I needed to be on something that wasn't moving around. Jacy and I relaxed in the van in the parking lot. Hakeem came back looking better with his head all wrapped up. He told us to hold off on the turban jokes till he could laugh also. As tired as everyone was, our good-byes to Florida were quick and to the point. He seemed rather short with the three knuckleheads, which to me was understandable. I thought his hugs and farewells to Jacy and I were genuine. The look in his eyes seemed to want to say more. He asked for my address and telephone number, which I thought was rather odd.

R and R

Chapter 26

With the few fish we caught in our coolers, we called my cousins Willie and Quinn, and headed over to their house in Hollywood. The sun was up by now, giving Quinn a reason to be fixing breakfast. Ordinarily, it would have been a thirty-minute drive to my cousin's house, but we got lost and had to call again to get help with directions. She came to the door with a granny-looking housecoat and hair fixed to match.

"What brings y'all down this way so early in the morning?" she asked, displaying her familiar bright smile and energetic tone. Before anyone could answer, she continued, "Looking like sunburned beach bums." We filed in the house one by one. "And whew!" she fanned the air. "Y'all know where the shower is."

"Ladies first," I said. "This is my girlfriend Jacy. Jacy, this is my cousin, Quinn." They said quick hellos before I led Jacy to the immaculately kept bathroom.

Hakeem came in last. Seeing Quinn staring at his bandages, he said, "Before you ask, I'll just say it's a long story. So let us settle down and we'll get around to telling it later, okay? Where's Big Daddy?" It's always been a running joke in the family that Quinn called her husband 'Big Daddy'. Hakeem was picking at her.

"You know he is in no hurry to get up. Besides, he hasn't been feeling too well the last couple of days. I think he's coming down with something. He kicks the covers off himself and the next minute he's talking about how cold he is. I'd say you could go stick your head in the door and say 'hey' but you might scare him right now with that thing on your head."

"To tell you the truth, Auntie, all I want to do right now

is lay down. I smell something in the kitchen, though. What's up?"

"You know how I do. It'll be ready in a minute. Y'all can come and get it when you get ready."

One by one, we hit the bathroom and gathered in the kitchen.

My cousin Willie is a tall man who worked hard physically before he retired. As close as I can figure, he's about 75, but in real good shape. We caught him by surprise when he walked in the room in his pajamas.

"Hey, Uncle Willie, how you doing?" Robbie asked, walking over to hug him. "Nice pajamas."

"Hey, Boy, what y'all doing back down here so soon?"

"Well, it's a long story. Aunt Quinn said you haven't been feeling too good. What's up, man?"

"I think I'm getting old. Boy it sucks, too. If you can help it, don't let it happen to you. Thang don't get hard when you want it to. Plus, every time you turn around, you gotta pee. That's why you see old men with their pants unzipped all the time. It ain't cause they forgot to zip'm up, it's 'cause you gotta pee so often it's easier to let'm stay open. Boy, get'n old sucks."

As long as I've known Willie, he's had a unique sense of humor. Piddling around in the kitchen, Quinn asked, "You feel like eating, Big Daddy?"

"Yeah, whatever you got left over is all right with me. Who's this pretty lady with y'all this time?"

I spoke up and took my turn to hug him. "Hey, Willie, good to see you. This is my girlfriend, Jacy Weber. She is from Jamaica."

"Jamaica? Well, that's all right. Hey sweetheart, any girlfriend of this boy is a girlfriend of mine."

Jacy chuckled. Willy extended his hand and said, "Our house is your house. Ain't no strangers here. I mean that now, you hear me?

"Nice to meet you sir. Me can call you 'Big Daddy' also?"

Jacy asked.

"No, sweetheart. You can call me anything else - Uncle Willie, Cousin Willy. But only my baby can call me Big Daddy. Tell her, Quinn, I think she trying to move in on your territory."

"Here, Willie, take my seat?" I offered.

"Naw man. I haven't been feeling too good. If I can get my baby to bring me a little something to eat, I'm gonna go back and lay down. You just take care of this pretty lady you got here, son."

"Don't worry, I will," I answered.

Willy got around to greeting Hakeem and asked, "Uh oh, you okay, boy?"

"Yeah, I'm gonna be all right, Uncle Willie. You the one been sick. You gonna be alright?"

"Yeah, I think I'm getting the flu. Looks like you banged your head up a little. You got to be more careful, son. You know you getting old too. You like these pajamas, too? My baby thinks I'm sexy in these things." Willie turned and headed back to his room. "Y'all make yourselves at home. I mean that, you hear me? I'll yell atcha later."

Quinn followed him back to the room with a plate of breakfast. When she came back, she asked, "Okay, Hakeem, why you wearing all them bandages on your head, and what y'all doing down here so early in the morning, and why y'all smelling like a hundred miles of bad road?"

"I got kicked in the head, Auntie. We just got back from a boat ride to Jamaica. And what was the last question? Oh, the same answer applies. We just got back from a boat ride to Jamaica."

"Robbie, does this have anything to do with that guy you were with the last time you were here?"

"Yeah, that's a friend of mine who owns a big fishing boat. We met on one of his trips in Jamaica and he invited me to go fishing with him if we were ever down this way. So when we were down here moving that guy back to Atlanta, I looked him up."

"Hey, Baby," Willie called from the end of the hall.

"Hang on for a minute, I am not letting y'all off the hook that easy." Quinn went to see what Willie wanted. When she came back, she sat back down and said, "Okay, keep talking."

"What you mean keep talking? That's pretty much it," Robbie countered.

"Like I said, keep talking."

Hakeem took over. "So the guy invited us to go the next time he went. We had a smooth trip down there, Auntie, but on the way back, the boat ran hot. We had to stop for a while out in the middle of the ocean. Gee got motion sickness, then on top of that, this other boat came and robbed us."

"Lawd have mercy." Quinn prayed. "And y'all got to fighting?"

"No, Auntie, there wasn't too much fighting. They had guns. I guess they wanted us to know they weren't playing. Me getting kicked was their way of showing it."

"Lawdy, lawdy, lawdy, I guess y'all won't be taking any more boat rides like that again," Quinn chuckled.

"I know I won't," Hakeem replied.

"I won't either," Robbie seconded. "So you know they got all our money."

"Lawdy, lawdy, lawdy." Quinn shook her head side to side sympathetically.

"So guess who we gonna ask for some gas money to get back to Atlanta?"

"Well, if that's the worse thing that happened, at least y'all lived to tell about it."

Like Willie suggested, we made ourselves at home for the rest of the day. It was a good opportunity to catch up on some sleep. Even though we weren't all alert and kicking, I think Quinn and Willy enjoyed seeing us. Unfortunately, Willie wasn't feeling his best because I know that he and his partner in crime, Hakeem, would have snuck off somewhere. Quinn and somebody went to the store to get some beer and groceries. Since we had brought some fresh fish, that's what was on the menu for dinner. My cousin always plays a good host when we see her. The next day we got up early, said our goodbyes, and hit the road back to Atlanta.

It was good to rest at Willie and Quinn's house. My body clock had been out of sync. Getting up early started me back on schedule. The nine-hour ride was routine and easy on everyone. A little more than two hours each behind the steering wheel made it easy. Our ride back was a little different with an extra body that happened to be female. Jacy's presence changed the usual 'man stuff' conversation. The atmosphere changed to an uneasiness everyone could feel, anyway. My boys had been flat, cold busted trying to smuggle marijuana back from Jamaica. So, with our fish on ice, a thick atmosphere between myself and the fellas, we made it back.

No Place Like Home

Chapter 27

I brought back more than an experience and some fish. I had an undocumented person and a revelation about the Three Stooges that prompted some changes. I had already decided that, even as close as the guys and I had been for the longest, their jeopardizing our freedom would cost them their jobs. That was a pretty tuff decision to make. Like Jacy said, 'I couldn't throw any first stones either.' I had also previously taken foolish chances in my life. But, at my age, I didn't need any more steps backward. I had too much to loose. In regard to Jacy, the U.S. is filled with illegal immigrants who function discretely and do well. The challenges we faced would be nothing new. Half the construction workers in the U.S. are undocumented, as are hotel housekeepers and lawn help. If they could function and be prosperous, with my help, Jacy could too.

Being back home was never so wonderful. I walked in and let go a big sigh of relief.

Jacy said, "Me can imagine how you feel. You don't tink dat when you left dat you'd be having anoder person coming back wit you."

"That was a sigh of relief, Baby. You know we don't appreciate what we got until it's either gone or close to being gone."

"Oh, what you mean?"

"That episode with the thieves on the boat was nearly fatal. They could have killed us and no one would have known anything about it."

"Me told you, Gee, dat Jah watch out for babes and fools."

197

"I hear ya, Jacy. You know I can look at you and sigh with relief also, because you were almost gone. So I have to stop, take a big breath and be thankful that you're still here. I appreciate you choosing me and you know what?"

"Eh?"

"As a result, I got you. Yup, as a result, you know I got you." I made up a song and started singing. "You know I got you, Oh, yes, I got you."

I took my impromptu song to another level, grabbed Jacy and started dancing.

"You know I got you.

Oh, yes, I got you. Nah-nah-nah-nah-nah-nah-nah. I got you."

"Gee, dat's de worst song me ever heard."

"I don't care.... Because I got you. I said I got you. Nah-nah-nah-nah-nah-nah-nah. I got you."

We both busted out giggling as I welcomed her to the house. Mocking my cousin Willy, I said "My house is your house. Ain't no strangers here. You hear me? I mean that now."

Jacy's wandering eyes gave her away. I could see that she was anxious to explore the house. After our dancing session in the living room, we went from room to room. She was like a kid in a candy factory taking in all the new stuff. If my perception of Jamaican life is like living in the past, Jacy was coming up to date. I had bought the house new a few years ago. It had a dishwasher, even though I never used it. It had four bedrooms, even though I didn't use them all. When we got to the master bedroom, I playfully grabbed her and fell on the bed. As I intended on giving her a full welcome, the phone rang. I let it ring but by the third time, realizing I had been out of town eight days, I caught it on the forth.

"Hello, may I help you?

"Yo, Gee? This is Chuck. How you doing?"

"Hey, man, how you doing?"

"How was your trip, boss, did you enjoy yourself?"

"Woo... Chuck, I don't know where to start. I'll just say there's no place like home."

"Aw, man, I hope everything is okay?"

"Everything is okay. How about you?"

"Well, I got some good news and some bad news."

With his statement came a bit of familiar anguish. I was back to the hassle of customers and employees. Hoping for the best but preparing for the worst I said, "Come on now, Big Chuck, I don't want to hear about any major calamities that happened while I was gone."

"No, bossman, it's nothing like that. One of the appointments you gave me before you left was moving a young lady from one Atlanta Housing Authority unit to another.

"Yeah."

"A new building had just been completed. As it turns out, the whole complex was being shut down. A representative of the Authority came as we were working and asked if we wanted to help with the other residents."

"Well, that's good news, Chuck, now give me the bad."

"The bad news is we've been working there almost nonstop since you been gone. I'm about beat. Gee, they got a hundred and fifty units to move ASAP."

"I hear ya, Big Chuck."

"I've done three a day for the last five days. So I kinda knew you guys would be getting back today and kinda committed the other three crews to help also. What you think about that, boss?"

"I think you 'kinda' did pretty good, Chuck. I appreciate you, Brotha. Sounds like you worked yourself up a raise. This is a big deal if we can get a chunk of that work."

"They do have access to other moving companies, but as long as we're on the property each day, we'll have work until all units are done."

"Well, the best we can do for them now is two crews,

mine and yours. Unfortunately Freddy, Robbie, and
Hakeem won't be helping anymore."

"What?"

"It's no big deal, Chuck, I'll just see you tomorrow
morning and we'll do what we gotta do. You say you been
working every day since I been gone?"

"Yes, Sir, bossman."

"Every day?"

"Every day."

"You the man, Chuck. I really appreciate you. I'll see you
tomorrow, first thing. Alright?"

"Alright."

During that short, two-minute conversation, Jacy had dozed off.
That gave me the opportunity to piddle around the house for a
while. Every time I leave there are certain things I have to do just to
feel 'at home' again. Gather my mail, water the plants, typical stuff
that needs immediate attention. With so much furniture moving to
be done, I was going to be real busy. I kept a list of guys who call me
from time to time looking for work. It would be easy to put together
another crew. That would make three to help knock out some of the
work Chuck stumbled upon. I was genuinely back to my old bump
and grind. Secure in the daily routine of things. It's good to work
and have something to do. With Jacy here, I really had things to do.
She didn't know it, but I had already included her in helping with
the moving service. Since there was something to do as early as
tomorrow, I let her sleep as I piddled around.

Leaving Hollywood this morning had put us back in Atlanta with an
appetite. Jacy slept for a good hour. I found some chicken hot dogs
in the freezer and doctored up some baked beans as I piddled.

"Hello, Sleeping Beauty." I woke her with the
announcement of, "Gee's Fine Dining and Catering
Service."

"Oh, how nice. What is it?"

"This is a Gee Howell special that will be so delightful to

your tongue that it'll make you wonder where I been all your life."

"Umm," she said as she took a spoonful of my barbecue-flavored beans. "Me like it."

"Oh, did you think you wouldn't? Here, try this. It's called a Danger Dog." I lifted it to her mouth and she took a bite.

With a mouthful of hotdog, we started laughing as she tried to talk. "Why you call it a Danger Dog?"

"Because my fingers will be in danger if I don't get them out of this dog's way."

"Me told you me get all de knuckleheads."

"No, Baby, I'm just different." We sat on the bed watching TV till the food was gone. We had fun acting silly and playing until eventually heading toward the shower. We finally went to bed to resume where we left off before Big Chuck called.

New Adventure

Chapter 28

If there is thrill in victory and agony in defeat, to endure a battle like the one with the thieves and come through it deserved celebrating. That brought us right to the edge; thank the Lord we didn't fall off. Florida shared the thrill of victory with the recovery of his mother. When teams win world championships, they celebrate by rejoicing together. I've never been on a world championship team, but I've experienced the camaraderie developed during such exultations. The results leave lifetime allegiances.

The first day found me back in my regular groove, meeting my men at seven-thirty in the morning. Jacy was right there with me. She was young and eager, so there was no reason for her to stay at home. There was nothing for her to do unless she wanted to fall into the stay-at-home-wife-syndrome. That didn't interest me. I didn't need that because I had been doing all those duties myself for years. Used to the labor intensive living in Jamaica, Jacy accepted the physical challenge. She didn't mind packing boxes and labeling items; she caught on very quickly. I kept an eye out to make sure she didn't do any heavy lifting. The first day got the best of her. There is a difference between office work and physical work. We laughed at how her muscles told her that she was out of shape. "Me hurt all over Gee," usually got her a full body massage in the evening, which was fine with me because it was the prelude to something else. "You're a savage!" she'd exclaim. We'd fall out and get up and do it again the next day. We worked steadily for the next week until I made headway on familiarizing a new group of fellas to my procedures.

As busy as we were, we had to make time to shop for clothes. There were things she needed immediately. "Even de grocery stores are different here, Gee," she said one day on the way home from work. I got a joy out of seeing Jacy's new experiences. We kept so busy as constant companions that two weeks passed like the blink of an eye. Each day brought a new surprise. The third week brought an even bigger one. I assumed a Florida post-marked envelope in the mail was from my cousins. It would be rather odd getting a letter from them, because we ordinarily talked by phone. The contents made me call Jacy to my office after I read the enclosed note.

"We got something from our boat friend Florida, Baby, that looks interesting."

"Yah, Mon."

"Here, you read it."

"No, Gee, you read it."

"Why I got to read it?"

"Oh! Me get all de knuckleheads." She proceeded to read.

"To Gee and Jacy,

I hope you had a safe trip back and everything is going okay with you guys. I wish I were there to enjoy some of that good Jamaican food that I know Jacy is fixing. Would you believe that after we got back I serviced the boat real good and headed back down to Capo the next day? For me to travel so much like that is nothing new. Remember I make a living with my boat. My mom has recuperated incredibly. It appears that she will have her wish of spending her last days or years, whatever the Lord allows her, in her home country. I have been trying to come up with some sort of way to show you and Jacy my appreciation. My father made some connections that I still have the benefit of. Enclosed you will find a birth certificate and a social security card that have been inserted into Florida's Health and Human Services Administration's record-keeping system. Feel free to use them as if Uncle Sam gave them to you himself. Trust me, he did, just a few years late. I hope the birth date is close enough for you to work with.

Your friend for life,

Clifford Williams."

I gazed at Jacy as tears formed in the corners of her eyes. "We really did risk a lot for paradise... but for us, it was worth it." I whispered, as we embraced.

Gerald Randolph Howard